Arise and Renew

Arise and Renew

Easter Reflections
for Adult Believers

Malcolm Cornwell, CP

The Liturgical Press
Collegeville, Minnesota

Cover by Janice St. Marie

Library of Congress Cataloging in Publication Data

Cornwell, Malcolm, 1940–
   Arise and renew.

   1. Easter—Meditations. 2. Paschal mystery—
Meditations. 3. Catholic Church—Doctrines—Meditations.
4. Bible. N.T. Gospels—Meditations. I. Title.
BV55.C66   1986   242′.36   85-24180
ISBN 0-8146-1441-8

Contents

To all those "who have gone before us marked with the sign of faith"

Eucharistic Prayer I

Acknowledgements

Any book is much more than the thoughts of its author in print. It is a sign of the encouragement and assistance of many people. This book is no exception. I am grateful in a special way to Brendan Keevey, Roger Gannon, and Lucian Clark, confreres and enablers all. Thanks also to Elaine Moore and Jeanette Beauchemin, who did the initial typing, and to Marion Dorscheimer, who assisted in the final preparation of the manuscript. To Bede Cameron, who proofread the text, and to Ed Mullaney and Ruth McGoldrick, whose helpful comments and gentle proddings helped make this book a reality, I am most thankful. Finally I must express gratitude to my parents, whose loyal support and continued interest in my life and work make labors like this an act of joyful praise.

Preface

Each year in the Easter feast the Church proclaims the resurrection of Christ and baptizes new members into the mystery of his dying and rising. At the lighting of the Easter candle, heralding the call to baptismal renewal for all believers, the Church cries out in faith, "May the light of Christ, rising in glory, dispell the darkness of our hearts and minds." Just as Christ has passed from the darkness of death to the glory of new life in resurrection, so too the Christian believer is challenged each year to renew the passage from the dark sleep of sin into the brightness of ever-increasing life and light. St. Paul, who instructs the Church on the meaning of baptism during Lent, recalled this image in a verse of an ancient hymn, "Awake, O sleeper, arise from the dead, and Christ will give you light" (Eph 5:14).

At the midpoint of the Lenten instruction for those preparing for baptism, the Church proclaims the Gospel of Christ giving sight to the man born blind. In this same gospel Jesus himself declares, "I am the light of the world" (John 9:5). On the night of the great vigil of Easter, those who have heard this gospel as a preparation for their baptism come forward to experience the power of this good news in a new and personal way. On this night both the candidates for baptism and the general faithful are called and challenged once again. Through the instruction of St. Paul during Lent, all have been reminded: "There was a time when you were darkness, but now you are light in the Lord. Well, then, live as children of light" (Eph 5:8). On the night of vigil, the Church proclaims to the joy of all, "Through baptism into his death we were buried with him, so that, just as Christ was raised from the dead by the glory of the Father, we too might live a new life" (Rom 6:4).

On this night the Gospel image of "Christ our Light" proclaimed and greeted in the first chant of the service becomes a new reality in the radiant faces of those baptized and made new in his name. It is a night for rebirth and exultation. No wonder the Church sings in jubilation: "This is the night when Christians everywhere, washed clean of sin and freed from all defilement, are restored to grace and grow together in holiness. This is the night when Jesus Christ broke the chains of death and rose triumphant from the grave." These words of the Easter Proclamation announce the beginning of a new day, a season of renewed life and increased faith in the risen Lord.

This book has one purpose in mind: to aid adult believers in the celebration of the Easter season. The event we call Easter is meant to be a renewing experience. To help us grow into this experience, the Church gives us not a day, but a season, a fifty-day jubilation to help us savor the meaning and the mystery of Christ's dying and rising. This season is an annual opportunity to rejoice in and reflect on the power of God's spirit at work in us. It is my hope that the reflections that follow will open many hearts to the possibility of new life in Christ during the Easter season and beyond.

Malcolm Cornwell
Easter 1985

Introduction

New and Growing Believers

Easter is resurrection, but Easter is also renewal. It is a call to every Christian heart: arise and renew! During the great vigil of prayer and rejoicing the Church calls new members to life in Christ. Their baptism on this evening is the high point of a long process of preparation called the catechumenate. This restored process of preparation for baptism of adults is becoming a sign or "sacrament" of Christ's universal call to conversion. It is a reminder to all believers that the goal of all Christian living is a constant rising to a new and evermore mature life in Christ.

The process leading to baptism is called the Rite of Christian Initiation of Adults (RCIA).[1] This process of adult catechesis and conversion envisions the season of Lent as a special time of intense preparation and instruction for those preparing for baptism at Easter.[2] It is being implemented with success and enthusiasm in many segments of the Church. In need of equal attention and emphasis is the celebration of the Easter season for all believers, both the newly baptized and the veteran members of the faithful. Here too the RCIA envisions a process and an experience, a time of celebration and reflection in which the newly baptized—those just received into full communion with the Church—their sponsors, and especially the general faithful share and experience once again the meaning of Christ's resurrection and their rising to new life in him.

A Season of Renewal and Mission

The Easter experience as described in the Rite of Adult Initiation is called the Period of Mystagogy. It is a time of postbaptismal instruction on the mysteries of Christian life.[3] It is a call to both the local faith community and the newly baptized to move forward together into the Easter season and to make the paschal mystery more a part of their lives, "by meditating on the Gospel, sharing in the Eucharist and doing works of charity" (RCIA #37). Just as the Lenten period of the catechumenate has become a "sacrament" of the call to adult conversion of heart, so too the Easter season, as outlined in the RCIA, is meant to unfold and strengthen the process of renewal in life and continued faith development. This season is also meant to become a "sacrament," a graced experience of new life. The Easter season is an image to the entire Church of what should constantly be going on among its members, namely the process of continual conversion through ongoing catechesis and continued growth in faith expressed in a willingness to serve.

The period of postbaptismal instruction is described as a time to unfold the mysteries of Christ and to experience and express the richness of life in him. It corresponds to the time of the great Easter sermons of Cyril, Ambrose, Augustine, and Chrysostom to their respective churches. The RCIA does not call us to repeat the catechetical methods of the third and fourth centuries but rather to discover for ourselves and our times how the newly baptized together with the faithful can reflect on and rediscover the power and unfolding experience of their baptismal life. Unlike the period of the catechumenate which is elaborately outlined and richly enhanced with rites and prayers, the RCIA merely presents the goals of the postbaptismal period, leaving the details and development of this Easter experience to the creativity and initiative of the Church.

Gathering the Faithful

The goals of this Easter experience are the same as the general goals of the catechumenate phase of initiation, the renewal of life. Step-by-step, complete initiation takes place in the midst of the community of the faithful. The overall goal of renewal of life in the total community can be accomplished most effectively in the Easter season by providing an opportunity for reflection and faith-sharing within the larger community. This fulfills the general goals of the entire Rite of Adult Initiation, which envisions that the veteran faithful along with the initiates will reflect with benefit upon the value of the paschal mystery, renew their own conversion, and by their example lead the members of the Church to obey the Holy Spirit with greater generosity and openness of heart.[4]

While the faithful have a role to play on behalf of the initiates, so too the new members play an important role in the overall renewal of the faith community. From the moment of baptism and full incorporation, Christian ministry begins. As catechumens and candidates for full communion, those seeking incorporation remind the faithful of the need for continual conversion; as new and full members they now stand in our midst as living reminders of the energy and enthusiasm of the Easter experience. This is expressed most clearly in the brief description of the Easter season contained in the RCIA: "The time of post-baptismal catechesis is of great importance so that the neophytes, helped by their sponsors, may enter into a closer relationship with *the faithful* and bring *them* a renewed vision and a new impetus" (RCIA #39—emphasis mine).

The Sunday assembly for Eucharist is recommended in the Rite as the place where ongoing instruction is to take place. Cycle A of the readings is always preferred, and the new members, along with their sponsors, are to have special places in the assembly as well as special mention in both the homily and the prayer of the faithful. At the close of the Easter season near Pentecost, and again on the anniversary of their baptism, a special celebration should be planned for the new members. This will help them share their faith with one another and strengthen their commitment.[5]

More Is Needed

While all of this is beneficial, it seems less than a desirable and effective conclusion to what has been envisioned by the RCIA itself, namely the renewal of the faith life of an entire local faith community. The Sunday assembly for Eucharist may well be the time of greatest attendance for the major part of that community, but the limitations of time and diverse levels of both presence and expectation hardly make it the optimum gathering place for the most effective implementation of the renewal experience envisioned for the Easter season.

During Lent the catechumens and candidates for full communion gathered with their sponsors for instruction and sharing. During the Easter season the same opportunity could be provided to augment the experience of the Sunday assembly. These gatherings, either on Sunday or another convenient evening, should be open to all who seek renewal in the Christian life. At the heart of these gatherings, the enthusiasm of the new members will bring a renewing energy to the Easter experience for all to share. This gathering of the new members and the veteran faithful is very much in accord with the spirit of the RCIA and its vision of the Easter season. These gatherings would provide an opportunity for all, new and veteran faithful alike, to share life and faith together and in that way begin to exercise ministry to each other.

The general outline suggested in the RCIA lends both structure and flexibility to the pastoral possibilities for this Easter experience. In addition to sharing in the Eucharist, the Rite recommends that the Easter season be a time for meditating on and sharing the meaning of the Easter message and gospel. Weekly gatherings for reflection, faith-sharing, and prayer would do a great deal to reawaken awareness at the heart of our Christian vocation, namely knowing Christ and sharing the power flowing from his resurrection (see Phil 3:10). Best of all this period of catechesis and renewal experience would be developed from the perspective of faith in the risen Christ, thus it would help restore Easter as the primary season for celebrating renewal of life in him.

Gospel Reflections

Keeping these goals in mind, the following chapters are a series of scriptural-liturgical reflections with a guide for personal reflection or group sharing. Each chapter is designed to be used by an individual reader or by a group of readers who may wish to share their reflections in an atmosphere of faith and communal prayer. In either case they are meant to draw the reader into the life-giving and faith-renewing experience of the Easter season.

Each chapter provides a reflection based on Scripture passages selected from the Lectionary of the Easter season, especially from the Gospel of John. Following each chapter and its reflection questions, there is a suggested prayer service. These prayer services are based on the theme of each chapter and are intended to help the reader enter more deeply into the mystery of the life we share with the risen Christ. These prayer services could be used for private prayer, but in line with the basic purpose of the book, they are arranged for group use under the guidance of a leader of prayer.

During the Easter season of renewal, the Church asks us to read the Gospel of John through the eyes of the Easter event and with the faith of a baptized believer. Viewed in this way the Easter Gospel presents a series of images of the Christ who is not only risen but ever new. Thus the Lectionary of the Easter season presents the Gospel of the risen Christ and the images he reveals to the Church in a way that is most suitable to the goals of the Easter experience outlined in the RCIA. These images, starting with the risen Lord himself, provide both the content and the challenge for our Easter reflection and the development of our faith. This experience should provide time to let the mystery of Christ unfold more completely in the lives of all the faithful and at the same time continue to bind the new members together with the veteran faithful into a renewed expression of the living body of Christ as Church. A desire for just such a process and experience is expressed in the opening prayer of the Church's liturgy for Easter Sunday:

> Let our celebration today raise us up and renew our lives by the Spirit that is within us.

This is a prayer not just for a day but for a season of life and faith, a season in which we are all called to arise and renew!

Notes

1. The Rites of Christian Initiation of Adults (RCIA), in *The Rites of the Catholic Church* (New York: Pueblo Publishing Company, 1976) 13–181, or *Christian Initiation of Adults,* in Liturgy Documentary Series #4 (Washington, D.C.: Office of Publishing Services, United States Catholic Conference 1983) 19–55. See also *Christian Initiation of Adults,* Study Text 10 (especially pages 67–77), published by the Conference in 1985.

2. RCIA #14–36.

3. RCIA #37–40.

4. RCIA #4.

5. RCIA #40, 235–38.

Chapter 1

A New Creation
The First Week of Easter

This is the day the Lord has made: let us rejoice and be glad. Alleluia!

Gospel Acclamation
Easter Octave

Each day during the first week of the Easter season, the Church proclaims this verse from Psalm 118. After inviting us to go back to the beginning of all things through a reflection on the work of creation at the vigil service, the Church now celebrates the Easter season which comes forth like a new creation. The dawn of this new day is the Risen Son, Jesus himself. Each day during this first week of our new beginning, the risen Christ appears in the gospel narrative to announce his presence and to share his gift of "Peace."

On Easter morning we joined the faithful women at the empty tomb to hear the announcement: "He is not here. He has been raised" (Matt 28:6).[1] With Peter and the beloved disciples we ran to the tomb and peered in to find it empty as was announced. Only the winding sheet lay in the empty hollow, and the cloth which had covered the head lay separately, rolled up in a place by itself (see John 20:6-7). This face veil was not dropped or left hurriedly as the winding clothes were; it was deliberately wrapped up and put aside. Like Moses who put aside his face veil when he ascended to meet God in glory, Jesus, the new Moses, has put aside the veil of his flesh and ascended to the glory of his Father. In this minute yet significant detail the Gospel of John gives us a "sign" of both resurrection and a call to glory. The face veils of the glorified Moses and of the resurrected Lazarus point us to the greater sign of the risen and glorious life which Jesus now enjoys. Like the beloved disciple peering into the empty tomb, we reflect on the evidence and begin to believe all over again.[3]

Soon signs give way to presence as the risen Jesus begins to appear in our midst in the gospel accounts proclaimed throughout the week. In the gospel tradition the resurrection is known not merely through the empty tomb but through the appearances of the risen Christ. It is through our reflection on these appearances that we begin to realize and experience that Jesus has not only gone to the Father in glory but has also returned to make us his bodily presence here and now. Jesus does this by sharing with us the gift of his abiding presence and Spirit which he promised.[4] For the Christian community there are no other gospel accounts that deserve the acclamation and response, "This is the Gospel of the Lord," and "Praise to you, Lord Jesus Christ," more than those announcing the resurrection.

"I am with you"

Through his resurrection Jesus is present with us in life, in community, and in worship. For well over twenty years now we have been growing into a new awareness of the many modes of Jesus' presence. The Constitution on the Sacred Liturgy of the Second Vatican Council reminded us of this fact, and our own developing sense of celebration is reinforcing the basic truth and experience of Jesus' promise, "Where two or three are gathered in my name, there am I in their midst" (Matt 18:20). Jesus is present to us in our assembly for worship, in sacramental signs, and in word.

"He is present in his word since it is he himself who speaks when the holy scriptures are read in the church."[5] During the Easter season, and especially the first week recalling the resurrection appearances of the Lord, there is a certain consistency to the word and message of Jesus. "Peace be with you" are the words he chooses to resume the dialogue with us, a dialogue that was painfully interrupted by his passion and death. Risen and alive, yet bearing the wounds which unite him even more completely to our human family, Jesus stands in our assembly and utters words only God could speak. He speaks a word of peace—"Shalom" (see Matt 28:9; Luke 24:36; John 20:19, 21).

Wherever God is, there is no room for fear, just awesome acceptance of the presence and the message. Here again there is a consistency in the message, announced first by the witnesses and then by Jesus himself, "Do not be afraid" (see Matt 28:10; Mark 16:6; Luke 24:38). God's presence is revealed to instill peace, not fear, and the risen Jesus quickly reminds our trembling hearts of this basic truth. This truth is revealed throughout the Word of God. It was the message at the heart of God's revelation to Moses at the burning bush. It was the consolation offered by so many of the Prophets. Angels announced it when they proclaimed the birth of the Messiah. Now Jesus himself, newborn from the tomb, manifests God's presence among us in spirit and in truth with the remarkable announcement that we need never be afraid. Jesus is risen from the dead and has appeared to reaffirm the truth of his word: "Take courage! I have overcome the world. I tell you all this, that in me you may find peace" (see John 16:33). Connected with this greeting of peace, a sense of urgency is conveyed in the command to bring this good news to others. The dialogue must continue!

Like all Christ's gifts his peace is meant to be shared with others. So too, his word, especially the word announcing his resurrection. In each of the gospels, the risen Lord makes this command quite clear: "Go and carry the news" (Matt 28:10); "Go into the whole world and proclaim the good news to all creation" (Mark 16:15); "You are witnesses of this" (Luke 24:48); and "As the Father has sent me, so I send you" (John 20:21).

"You are witnesses"

In us and through us, the risen Jesus continues his dialogue of life-giving presence to others. This is the wonder of Christianity: Jesus Christ who was crucified is risen, and his life, his word, and his presence live on in those he has named his witnesses. The very presence of a Christian, a baptized believer in Jesus Christ, is meant to be an announcement to the world that "He is risen!" No wonder Jesus said to Mary Magdalene, whom he called by name in the garden of the new creation, "go to my brothers and tell them, 'I am ascending to my Father and your Father, to my God and your God!' " (John 20:16-17). Mary went and did as the risen Christ commanded, but before she announced his message, she proclaimed her personal witness, "I have seen the Lord!" (John 20:18).

Alone, our witness and experience sometimes seems feeble and weak. Together as Church, as a body of believers, it is a strong and firm foundation upon which to build. There is nothing stronger than a faith which is shared and proclaimed together. This is true in all areas of Christian life and experience. It is true of our personal and communal prayer. It is true when we hear and respond to God's word together in the Scriptures. And it is certainly true when we assemble together to make the signs of Jesus' presence in sacrament, especially the sign of the breaking of the bread.

When believers come together as Church, Jesus keeps his promise to be with us in a special way. Nowhere is this more concretely experienced than in our assembly for Word and sacrament. This is highlighted in the first week of the

Easter season through the story of the walk of the two disciples to the village of Emmaus. This event is a gem of catechetical wisdom and a mirror reflecting the experience of our own pilgrim journey in the Christian life.

Our Personal Journey

A reading of Luke 24:13-35 will evoke for us our own sense of journey, indeed our own story. On Easter two disciples were walking back to their village of Emmaus after the events of the past three days. They had heard the "tale" of Christ's resurrection, but the impact of its meaning had not yet touched their hearts. As an unrecognized yet willing companion, the risen Lord joins their journey and listens to their conversation. How beautifully Luke describes Christ's presence to them, "Jesus approached and began to walk along with them" (Luke 24:15).

Accepting them and the present stage in their life's journey, Jesus begins his ministry to them simply by listening. In fact he evokes conversation by showing interest in their dilemma and discussion, "What are you discussing as you go your way?" (Luke 24:17). Their response is filled with irony and even a touch of humor. They tell Jesus about the hope they had in the one who was crucified, died, and was buried. Now, they tell him, there is a rumor he is risen. They are telling Jesus *the good news!* Yet in their mouths the Gospel message of the Church's creed is not yet an act of faith. It does not give life.

How often have we mouthed the good news, or recited the basic summary of our faith with little or no effect? "For our sake he was crucified under Pontius Pilate; he suffered, died, and was buried. On the third day he rose again in fulfillment of the Scriptures."[6] Easter brings these words into focus once again, and the risen Lord challenges us to let them burn in our hearts anew. "How slow you are to believe" (Luke 24:25). Knowing the slow pace of our progress in faith, Jesus will once again instruct us in the Scriptures during the journey of the Easter season. "Beginning, then, with Moses and all the prophets, he interpreted for them every passage of Scripture which referred to him" (Luke 24:27). How privileged they were to have Jesus open their minds and hearts to his presence through the Word. How privileged we are who also have the presence of the Lord as we journey throughout life. After all, what is our prayer if not a conversation with Christ? What is our reading or our reflective hearing of the Word if not an opportunity to meet the Lord on the pathways of life? Both are opportunities for growing in faith. Both are moments capable of opening us to the experience of his presence. "Were not our hearts burning inside us as he talked to us on the road and explained the Scriptures to us?" (Luke 24:32).

Moved by his words, the two disciples invited their companion to stay with them. "So," as the gospel beautifully announces and sets the scene, "he went in to stay with them" (Luke 24:29). No sooner did they sit at table, when Jesus assumed the principal role. "He took bread, pronounced the blessing, then broke the bread and began to distribute it to them" (Luke 24:30). At the sight of these familiar gestures, their eyes were opened, their hearts responded, and they recognized the risen Jesus as their companion at table. Seeing the familiar gestures of the breaking of the bread once again prompted them to reflect on all the other times Jesus had done the same thing. He had broken bread with tax collectors and outcasts in Levi's house. He shared bread with the multitudes in the countryside. It is most likely he did so at the meal in the home of a leading Pharisee, when he taught his message of humility and acceptance of others. Most recent was their memory of what he did on the night before he died (see Luke 5:27-32; 9:12-17; 14:1-11; 22:14-20). On that night Jesus transformed the meaning of the bread. He so identified it with himself that he said, "This is my body to be given for you" (Luke 22:19). Now here he was again at table with them in their own village of Emmaus. "Thus evening came, and morning followed—the first [new] day" (Gen 1:5).

New Life, New Meaning

If Jesus has the creative power to transform the meaning of bread, he also has the power to transform lives. In the Emmaus story that is exactly what he did. The two disciples were certainly changed after their encounter with the risen Lord. Before their contact with him, they were downcast and dejected; after they were buoyed up and filled with belief. Because of Christ the meaning of their lives had changed.

Because of Christ and our baptism into him the meaning of our lives has also changed. We are a new creation. In him a new day is continually dawning. We are growing and developing in him through faith. That is the meaning of discipleship, a never ending process of development and growth in our response to Christ's continual call to follow him. The Emmaus story is so consoling and life-giving. The two pilgrims were disciples of Jesus. They had heard his call and known his presence, and despite the darkness and discouragement of their present moment, they were willing to begin once again. The spark of his life was rekindled in their hearts once they recognized Christ's presence in their midst.

We too are disciples of the Lord, and yet from time to time our vision becomes blurred, and our journey in faith seems to slow down to a crawl. But because of Christ's presence in our prayerful conversations with him and his presence in Word, sacrament, and other believers, we too can know renewing moments when the spark of his life is rekindled in our hearts. It is in these moments that the same dull road of our life's journey becomes an open highway spurring us on to fulfill our call as his disciples and witnesses. Like the renewed disciples of the Emmaus story, we too can recount what has happened on our road and how we have come to know Jesus not only in the breaking of bread but in every experience of his risen presence.

The Gospel of the risen Christ gives ample witness that as his disciples we too will experience his presence when we share our story and journey together. Whether in the midst of life's journey, at the meal of his table, or in a refreshing moment of sharing the experience of his life-giving presence with others, disciples in every age can cry out and give witness to their common faith in Christ. "The Lord has been raised! It is true! He has appeared to . . . ." (Luke 24:34).

Texts for Reading

Matthew 28:8-15	Jesus' greeting of peace
Mark 16:9-15	Proclaim the good news
Luke 24:13-35	Jesus is recognized in Word and meal
John 20:1-19	He is risen and calls us by name

Suggestions for reflection and/or discussion:

The good news is that "he is risen!" The resurrection appearances of Jesus recounted in the gospel image to the faithful his life and work among us.

1. How do I know and experience the presence of the risen Lord in my life?
2. Recall the story of your own journey with Jesus. Write it out or tell it to another person.
3. At what times in my journey have I most clearly recognized the presence of the risen Lord?

Suggested Prayer Service

Opening song:	Jesus Christ Is Risen Today Alleluia, Sing to Jesus Ye Sons and Daughters (select one from a common hymnal)
Psalm:	Psalm 118 or Psalm 16
	Psalms can be celebrated in a variety of ways: —one person reads slowly; —all recite, alternating stanzas in two groups; —use a sung or spoken antiphon while one

person renders the psalm. Alleluia is always an appropriate antiphon.

Reading: Acts 10:34-43 or 1 Corinthians 15:1-11

Pause for reflection

Call to prayer:

We are an anointed people signed with the cross of Christ. At the hearing of his good news, we bring our mind and our heart to receive Christ and our lips to proclaim him. Let us pray:

Petitions:

Through the sign of the cross received on our forehead, may we come to know and follow Christ, the light of the world.
    R. Lord, hear our prayer.

Through the sign of the cross received on our lips, may we faithfully proclaim and respond to Christ, the Word of God.
    R. Lord, hear our prayer.

Through the sign of the cross received on our hearts, may we always walk with Christ, the source of our life and our love.
    R. Lord, hear our prayer.

(During the petitions the gesture of making the sign of the cross on the senses might accompany the prayer. This is the same gesture we make before the hearing of the gospel at the Eucharist.)[7]

All recite: The Lord's Prayer

Concluding prayer:

Author of life, during this Easter season you give us the joy of recalling the resurrection of Christ to newness of life. May our sharing in this annual renewal of faith help us to put into action the baptism we have all received. We ask this through Christ our Lord.
    R. Amen.

Exchange a greeting of peace.

Notes

1. Gospel Reading: Matt 28:1-10, the Easter Vigil: Cycle A; see also Mark 16:1-8, Cycle B; Luke 24:1-12, Cycle C.

2. Gospel Reading: John 20:1-19, Easter Sunday: Cycle A, B, C.

3. The face veil is a sign of Christ's resurrection and our call to glory in the risen Lord. See Sandra M. Schneiders, I.H.M., "The Face Veil: A Johannine Sign," *Biblical Theological Bulletin* XIII, no. 3 (July 1983) 96.

4. See John chapters 14 and 16 on the role of the Spirit-Paraclete. This will be developed later in chapter 6.

5. *The Conciliar and Post-conciliar Documents,* ed. Austin Flannery, O.P., (Collegeville, Minn.: The Liturgical Press, 1975). See The Constitution on the Liturgy #7, 5.

6. The Nicene Creed. The Creed is given to those seeking full initiation as a summary of faith (RCIA #183-187). The content of the Creed is part of the formula for the renewal of baptism by all the faithful at the Easter Eucharist.

7. These actions and petitions are modeled on the rite for the blessing of the senses, see RCIA #83-85.

Chapter 2

Jesus, Life and Light
The Second Week of Easter

In the tender compassion of our God the dawn from
on high shall break upon us, to shine on those who dwell
in darkness and the shadow of death, and to guide our feet
into the way of peace.

Canticle of Zachary from Morning Prayer

The Easter Gospel is not only the Scripture passage
selected by the Church to announce the resurrection of Christ
on Easter day. The Easter Gospel is the entire gospel of the
season, all of the selections of good news presented to us
for reflection and response during this time for celebrating
new life. Through the selection and arrangement of certain
texts for the Lectionary, the Church is making a statement
about our faith in the risen Lord. In a very real sense we
are being given another gospel, a new look at the Jesus we
have come to know and believe from the writings of the four
evangelists. In the seasons of the liturgical year, the Church
itself becomes an evangelist, both proclaiming and inviting
response to the Jesus whose presence we encounter in our

assembly for worship. In the Easter season we hear and experience once again the voice and presence of the risen Lord calling us to himself and challenging us to renewal of life.[1]

The week of the resurrection appearances is completed. Now a new day and a new week have begun. The second Sunday of Easter is the eighth day of the new creation. The appearances of Jesus were not an illusion. Like the eternal dawn of a new day, the risen Lord stands once again in our midst, filling our lives with his message of peace. He again reassures us of his presence by showing his hands and his side. Once more his greeting echoes in our ears and quickens our spirits: "Peace be with you" (John 20:21).

This time, however, the risen Lord gives us even more cause for rejoicing. He speaks to us saying, "As the Father has sent me, so I send you." Then he breathes on us and says, "Receive the Holy Spirit" (John 20:21-22). Here the risen Jesus, author of the new creation, stands in our midst, sharing the very gift he has received from the Father through resurrection: life, breath, and the Spirit itself. Just as God, the Creator, shared the breath of life with all creatures in the first creation, now Jesus shares the breath of eternal life with his disciples in the new creation (see Gen 2:7). As Jesus was sent to give witness to God's promise of new and eternal life, now we are sent to be witnesses to that life through the gift of the same Spirit that raised Jesus from the dead. In a dramatic gesture Christ breathed on his disciples to share his life and mission with them. This is what the Church has done to us when we were reborn in Christ through baptism. Like the first disciples we have been called to share in the power and spirit of Jesus Christ. We have been sent to give witness by faith to his life and his love.

Two Witnesses

During this second week of the Easter season, we meet two people, Thomas and Nicodemus, who come forth from the Gospel of John to help us reflect on the mystery of our faith in Christ. Thomas comes doubting, yet seeking signs, and meets the Lord, who is present in a community of faith.

Nicodemus comes to Christ believing in signs and moves to a deeper level of faith and a commitment to service within the community. Both of these believer-disciples bear the marks of rebirth in Christ. Of these two witnesses Thomas is perhaps the more familiar and kindred spirit.

How often like Thomas do we feel we have missed out, that something is lacking in our experience of faith? There are times when others around us seem to be on a different level of faith than the one we now know. The Gospel story of the Lord's understanding manner with Thomas is a comfort in times of doubt or when we feel a lack of growth. In times like these, the risen Jesus quietly stands in our midst and waits for the moment when we become aware of his presence and his gift of peace in a new way. Then as with Thomas before us, he accepts our act of faith, "My Lord and my God!" (John 20:28). It is in those moments that our faith is confirmed within the community of believers who have been telling us, "We have seen the Lord!" (John 20:25). It is then that we receive the blessing of Christ who reminds us that Thomas became a believer because he saw the risen Lord, but "Blest are they who have not seen and have believed" (John 20:29). Unlike the Magdalene and Thomas, whose unique experience of the Lord was to know him in the fleshly appearance of his risen body, the more common and normative experience of believers is the recognition of Christ's presence in the community of faith, his body the Church. This body, gifted with his life and Spirit, continues to give voice to the apostolic witness, "We have seen the Lord." That is always good news (see John 20:19-29).

The Gospel of John ends with the blessing of all believers and a brief reference to many unrecorded signs which Jesus performed in the presence of his disciples. The signs that are recorded in the Gospel are given to foster faith in Jesus so that through him the believer may have life in his name (see John 20:29-31).[2] This reference to the many other signs performed by Jesus makes a good transition to another expression of faith in our celebration of this second week of Easter, that of Nicodemus. A reading of his encounter with the Lord will prove helpful. It is contained in John 3:1-21.

From Darkness to Light

Nicodemus was a good man. He was a faithful Jew and a respected member of the Sanhedrin. He was a recognized religious leader in his day. Perhaps out of fear of being recognized or of being misunderstood, he came to Jesus by night. Nevertheless, he came, and despite the darkness he was seeking light while proclaiming the truth. In his own way Nicodemus tells us he is already a believer in Jesus. "We know you are a teacher come from God, for no man can perform signs and wonders such as you perform unless God is with him" (John 3:2). Nicodemus' faith is real, but incomplete. It is based on signs; later it will be based on Jesus himself. But Nicodemus is on the right track, since he clearly recognizes the reason Christ's signs have power is that "God is with him" (John 3:2). That is always the reason for faith in Jesus, our recognition that God is present in his word and deeds.

Nicodemus calls the words and deeds of Jesus signs. For him they manifest God's presence. In the unfolding of John's Gospel, as it is written, Nicodemus is referring to the first of the signs which Jesus performed. It was at Cana in Galilee. The sign was the water which flowed as rich vintage wine, a sign which Jesus linked with the "hour" of his passion, death, and resurrection to glory. This was the hour when the Spirit of Jesus would flow like new wine into the hearts of all who would believe and receive it (see John 2:4).[3]

The story of the meeting of Nicodemus with Jesus is the beginning of the Church's reading of the Gospel of John during the Easter season. Because of this the scene takes on a special significance for a baptized believer in Jesus. The signs which influenced Nicodemus' faith include the ones we have witnessed during our observance of the Lenten season as a preparation for baptism or its renewal in our lives. These signs include the giving of sight to the man born blind and the raising of Lazarus from death to new life (see John 9:1-41; 11:1-45).[4] Both these signs are images of the effects of our baptism into Christ, who is the light and life of the world. Thus when Nicodemus comes to Jesus in our celebration of the Easter season, he comes seeking light and life from a Jesus in whom we already believe. What then can Nicodemus teach us? The answer is simple: faith can and does grow both in depth and in expression.

This is clearly the teaching of our ever renewing Church. Christian life and faith begin at baptism, but it is just a beginning. Baptism is the beginning of a process of rediscovering and developing the life of Christ within us. Faith is the expression and experience of that life, and like all life it needs to be nourished in order to grow. This nourishment comes from continuous contact with Christ through his body the Church. Baptism is the beginning of this contact. The rest of our Christian life is the unfolding of its effects. Baptism is the unfolding of our life of faith in Jesus Christ. That is why at the beginning of the baptismal ritual, in response to the question, "What do you ask of the Church?" the answers "baptism" or "faith" are both acceptable. They are both expressions of a desire for life in Christ.[5] Through the ceremony of baptism, we were united with Christ. Through the journey of our life of faith, we continue to experience the effects of that union. By baptism we were "grafted into the paschal mystery of Christ," we were united with him in death to sin and raised up to live a new life.[6]

The Teaching of the Second Vatican Council

Through the great Magna Charta of renewal, the Constitution on the Church, we the people of God are still being called to a renewed appreciation of our personal Christian dignity. This document, which hails Christ as the Light to the Nations, reminds us of the centrality of baptism in the life of the Church. Christ himself "asserted the necessity of faith and baptism (see Mark 16:16; John 3:5) and thereby affirmed at the same time the necessity of the Church, which we enter through baptism as through a door.''[7] United with Christ we form a body of believers consecrated to the witness of faith and the worship of God. In this common bond we exercise what the Council has called ''the priesthood of the faithful.''[8]

In speaking of the great mystery of the Church, the Second Vatican Council has drawn on the Scriptural images which help to develop our understanding of who we are as God's people. We are a sheepfold whose only gateway is Christ; a field of God's land ready for cultivation; a building made from the living stones of our lives whose cornerstone is Christ.[9] Christ is central to the Church and to our lives. He is the focus of faith and everything else flows from him. Our baptism has united us with Christ in a unique and undeniable way. Through baptism we have become a single body in Christ. In him we share one table of word and Eucharist for instruction and nourishment, one ministry of service to build up his body, the Church.[10] This is the great mystery and dignity we share as a people, consecrated to God and bonded together through baptism in Jesus Christ. By the power of the risen Lord in our midst, we are given strength to overcome human weakness and to show forth to the world the mystery of his presence among us in a real yet shadowed way, until at last it will be revealed in clearer light and total glory.[11]

This language of growth and development used to describe the Church and our lives as members of Christ's body is most reflective of the times in which we live. We are very conscious of growth and development in our personal life. Why not also in the area of our life of faith? That is meant to grow and develop too! This is exactly why Nicodemus is so important. He is a model of growth in faith and commitment to Christ. He shows us we are never too old to learn or to grow.

Nicodemus in Another Light

Most likely Nicodemus was a person in midlife. He had achieved a measure of success and respect. It was a risk for him to reach out and seek instruction from the young rabbi,

Jesus. Perhaps that is why he came to him by night. The dialogue which follows is a masterpiece of Gospel instruction. It is much more than a dialogue between two rabbis; it becomes a discourse by Jesus on the meaning of the Christian life. Nicodemus makes three statements, and to each one Jesus gives an increasingly longer response. Each response is a solemn assurance of divine truth.

Nicodemus recognizes God's work in the signs Jesus performs. Jesus assures him that no one can even be aware of this unless he is begotten from above. Jesus is encouraging Nicodemus in the life of faith. Taking Jesus much too literally, Nicodemus questions him about this begetting in his now famous question about being born again. Jesus replies that it is not human rebirth he is talking about—"Flesh begets flesh"—but rather rebirth into the divine life, a new birth, begotten from above, when "Spirit begets spirit" (John 3:6).

This regeneration is the work of the Holy Spirit. It takes place through the action of water and the Spirit. The mention of water brings this dialogue with Nicodemus and the Old Law to the level of the Christian believer and New Testament. It is here that the true teaching of the discourse begins to emerge and flow. From this point on Jesus speaks more like a mature Christian catechist instructing a developing Church community than like a young rabbi at the beginning of his public ministry. In the Old Testament water and the spirit were linked as a sign of new life and covenant with God; now Jesus speaks about water in the Church's New Testament understanding of the sacrament of baptism and its new covenant significance (see Isa 55:1-11; Ezek 36:16-28).[12] Baptism gives us new life in Jesus, and the gift of the Spirit enables us to know and believe in his teaching (see John 14:26; 16:14-15). So it is, Jesus says, with everyone "begotten from above . . . begotten of the Spirit" (John 3:7-8). They become not only new born but growing believers.

"If I am lifted up"

Nicodemus' final question is brief and to the point, "How can such a thing happen?" (John 3:9). But Jesus' reply is the longest and most solemn part of his discourse. Here he is speaking as the risen Lord of Glory who has been "lifted up" and now bestows eternal life on all who believe in him. The statement about the Son of Man being "lifted up" is the first of three such statements in the Gospel of John. They correspond to the three predictions of the passion found in the other Gospels (see John 3:14; 8:28; 12:32-34).[13] In the Gospel of John, the lifting up of Jesus refers not only to his being lifted up to die on the cross but also to his being lifted up to glory through resurrection and ascension to the Father. This glorious lifting up of Jesus began the communication of the gift of the Spirit which John clearly associates with the waters of baptism. "If anyone thirsts, let him come to me; let him drink who believes in me" (John 7:37-38). "Here," John says, "he was referring to the Spirit, whom those that came to believe in him were to receive. There was, of course, no Spirit as yet, since Jesus had not yet been glorified" (John 7:39). Jesus clearly tells us that he has given his life not only *for* us but *to* us forever and that this is because God loves the world so much (see John 3:16).

From Light to Life

Jesus is the light of the world. To believe in him is to follow the light; to reject him and not believe is to walk in darkness. Like Nicodemus we have walked from darkness to light, from the dim shadows of disbelief into the radiant light of faith in the risen Christ. Like Nicodemus we are willing to learn and to grow. For us Nicodemus is a model disciple, one who is willing to walk with Christ and to grow in faith.

The Gospel of John does not abandon Nicodemus at the scene of his nighttime visit to Jesus; he appears briefly on two more occasions, and each time he gives evidence of more light and more life. He is a living testimony to the assurance of Jesus that "he who acts in truth comes into the light, to make clear that his deeds are done in God" (John 3:21).

During the harvest feast of Booths, Jesus went up to Jerusalem and began to teach in the temple courtyard. A controversy arose over him, while some came to believe in him. Finally the chief priests and the Pharisees sent the temple guard to arrest Jesus, but instead they listened to his teaching and returned to testify that "no man ever spoke like that before" (John 7:46). Their testimony was in reference to Jesus' invitation "If anyone thirsts, let him come to me" (John 7:37). After a warning from the Sanhedrin not to be taken in by his teaching and that no one among their number believed in Jesus, Nicodemus stood up to say, "Since when does our law condemn any man without first hearing him . . . ?" (John 7:51). Nicodemus who has heard and now believes wants others to hear Jesus for themselves. His faith has grown stronger through the Word of the Lord.

Finally Nicodemus appears for the last time on what seems to be the last day of Jesus' life. When the Light is snuffed out, Nicodemus catches his spark. Nicodemus emerges as a disciple, a believer, who comes forth to do the truth in love. The passage is worth quoting in full. It is the conclusion of the Passion of Jesus read on Good Friday:

> Afterward, Joseph of Arimathea, a disciple of Jesus (although a secret one for fear of the Jews), asked Pilate's permission to remove Jesus' body. Pilate granted it, so they came and took the body away. Nicodemus (the man who had first come to Jesus at night) likewise came, bringing a mixture of myrrh and aloes which weighed about a hundred pounds. They took Jesus' body, and in accordance with Jewish burial custom bound it up in wrappings of cloth with perfumed oils. In the place where he had been crucified there was a garden, and in the garden a new tomb in which no one had ever been buried. Because of the Jewish Preparation Day they buried Jesus there, for the tomb was close at hand (John 19:38-42).

As the sun was setting, and a new day and a new creation were about to dawn, Nicodemus, "the man who had first come to Jesus by night," comes forth to perform an act of love and service. He anoints and helps bury the body of Christ. From a tiny spark his faith has grown into an uncontainable fire. He has indeed come into the light!

St. Nicodemus, pray for us.

Texts for Reading

John 20:19-31	Receive the Holy Spirit
John 3:1-21	Jesus' dialogue with Nicodemus and all believers

Suggestions for reflection and/or discussion:

The Easter mysteries of Jesus have released his Spirit into our lives. Baptism is the beginning of a whole lifetime of growth in both the experience and expression of faith.

1. How do I experience the Spirit of Jesus as light, as life, as truth?
2. How does my interaction with other believers increase my own faith?
3. Does the Spirit of Jesus bring light when I find myself in doubt or darkness again?
4. Do I find myself coming forth into the light as a minister to the Body of Christ?

Suggested Prayer Service

Light a candle and pause for silence.

Leader: Jesus Christ is the light of the world.

Response: Amen.

Psalm: Psalm 27

Reading: Colossians 1:12-20

Pause for reflection

Call to prayer:

We are a people enlightened by Christ. By the power of his Cross and the waters of baptism, we have conquered sin and death and are rising to new and eternal life. Let us invoke those who have gone before us marked with the sign of faith:

> Lord, have mercy,
> > Lord, have mercy.
> Christ, have mercy,
> > Christ, have mercy.
> Lord, have mercy,
> > Lord, have mercy.
> Holy Mary, Mother of God,
> > pray for us.
> Adam and Eve,
> > pray for us.
> Abraham, our father in faith,
> > pray for us.
> Isaiah, the prophet,
> > pray for us.
> Ezekiel, the visionary,
> > pray for us.
> Man, born blind,
> > pray for us.
> Martha and Mary,
> > pray for us.
> Risen Lazarus,
> > pray for us.
> Joseph of Arimathea,
> > pray for us.

Nicodemus,
> pray for us.

Women at the tomb,
> pray for us.

Mary of Magdala,
> pray for us.

Simon Peter,
> pray for us.

Thomas, the doubter,
> pray for us.

Beloved Disciple,
> pray for us.

Paul of Tarsus,
> pray for us.

Christ, hear us,
> Christ, hear us.

Lord Jesus, hear our prayer,
> Lord Jesus, hear our prayer.

Recite the Lord's Prayer

Final Prayer:

God of mercy, you have filled us with light and life. May we, who celebrate our rising to new life in Christ, be helped in our journey by the prayers of those who have gone before us marked with the sign of faith. We ask this through Christ, our Lord. Amen.

Closing Song (suggestions):   The Light of Christ

The Lord Is My Light[14]

We Are the Light of
the World[15]

NOTES

1. Eugene LaVerdiere, S.S.S., *The New Testament in the Life of the Church* (Notre Dame, Ind.: Ave Maria Press, 1980) 143–47. Father LaVerdiere states that "taken together the season's gospel readings constitute the church's own Advent, Lenten, Christmas or Easter Gospel, each of which is as distinctive as the Gospel narratives according to Matthew, Mark, Luke and John." It is in the Easter Season that the Church "celebrates the resurrection and examines its implications for Christian life" (144–45).

2. John 20. This is the original conclusion of the Gospel as intended by the author. Chapter 21 is an accepted addition to the original text.

3. See also John 12:23-28; 13:1 for the "hour" of Jesus.

4. These two Gospel selections are from the A Cycle for the Fourth and Fifth Sundays of Lent. Together with the dialogue of Jesus and the Samaritan woman (John 4:4-42) for the Third Sunday of Lent, they comprise the three great baptismal images used by the Church in the instruction of adult candidates preparing for the sacraments at Easter.

5. See *The Rites:* The Rite of Baptism for Children #37, 198; The Rite of Christian Initiation for Adults #75, 41.

6. Flannery, The Constitution on the Liturgy #6, 7.

7. Flannery, The Constitution on the Church #14, 365–66.

8. *Ibid.* #10, 11, 360–63.

9. *Ibid.* #6, 353–54.

10. *Ibid.* #7, 355.

11. *Ibid.* cf. #8, 357–58.

12. These passages are among those selected from the Old Testament for the Easter vigil.

13. See also the predictions of the passion in Mark: Mark 8:31; 9:31; 10:33-34.

14. See *Songs of Praise,* Volume I #52, 54 (Ann Arbor, Mich.: Servant Music).

15. See *People's Mass Book* (New Edition) #152 (Schiller Park, Ill.: World Library Publications).

Chapter 3

Jesus, Companion and Nourishment
The Third Week of Easter

Man does not live on bread alone, but on every word that comes from the mouth of God, Alleluia.

Gospel Acclamation
Monday of the Third Week of Easter

All of the four gospels agree that one of the most significant events in the life of Jesus was his feeding of the multitudes with a few loaves of bread. They all agree on what Jesus did with the loaves: he *took* them, *blessed* or gave thanks over them, *broke* them, and *gave* them either directly to the people or to his disciples for distribution to the crowds (see Matt 14:13-21; Mark 6:30-44; Luke 9:10-17; John 6:1-13). These key words describing the gestures and prayer of Jesus on this occasion have been taken over by the Church in fulfilling his command at the Last Supper, "Do this in memory of me."[1] Each time we celebrate the Eucharist we recall what Jesus did on the night before he died. The words of the Fourth Eucharistic Prayer recall this event with the flavor of the Gospel of John.

He always loved those who were his own in the world. When the time came for him to be glorified by you, his heavenly Father, he showed the depth of his love. While they were at supper, he took the bread, said the blessing, broke the bread and gave it to his disciples saying: Take this, all of you, and eat it: This is my body which will be given up for you.

These words and the prayerful gestures that accompany them are not only the fulfillment of Jesus' command but of the Church's faith in the person of Jesus who said, "I myself am the bread of life" (John 6:35). In this bold and direct statement Jesus has not only declared himself to be present in the bread of our Eucharistic celebrations but more directly he is saying that he himself is the only satisfying nourishment for our human hungers. When Jesus says in our Easter Gospel that he is "the bread of life," the emphasis is not on the bread as such, but on himself as the "I" who declares it. What Jesus is saying is that what we long for to nourish our hungers is to be found in the "I" who has personally identified his life with the bread he gives (see John 6:51).[2] Jesus is more than mere bread for our bodily hunger. He is more than love to satisfy our emotional needs. He is the word that will satisfy our hunger for truth. He is bread for life itself; the total satisfaction for all our human hungers.

The Easter Gospel

The use of John's bread of life discourse during the Easter season is a key part of the Church's catechesis on the mysteries of Christ. The image of Jesus as the bread of life is at the heart of what the period of mystagogy is all about. This image of the bread of life and the events we have recalled in the Emmaus story combine to form another segment of our Easter Gospel. In this Gospel the risen Lord becomes our companion in our journey and at our table. He is as the word alludes, "cum-panis," with us as bread, our food and nourishment for the journey of life. Like the pilgrim disciples of the first Easter evening, we have "come to know him in the breaking of bread" (Luke 24:35). For all baptized believers, new and old alike, the Eucharist is the primary way of celebrating and sustaining contact with the risen Lord. The stories of the resurrection appearances of Jesus picture him sharing in several meals with his disciples: at the table of Emmaus, in the upper room at Jerusalem, and on the lakeside in Galilee.[3] These post-resurrection meal stories confirm the testimony of Peter, who openly proclaimed that the disciples of Jesus "ate and drank with him after he rose from the dead" (Acts 10:41). This testimony is proclaimed to all the faithful every Easter Sunday as the first reading in the Eucharistic assembly.[4]

Jesus, the I AM

In the bread of life discourse Jesus speaks on many levels of meaning. Just as he did using the image of water in the discourse with Nicodemus, Jesus now summons those who believe in him to a deeper level of awareness of his presence with the image of bread. Jesus reminded those who first heard his words, "It was not Moses who gave you bread from the heavens; it is my Father who gives you the real heavenly bread" (John 6:32). In this statement Jesus recalls the image of Moses and the gift of the manna in the desert. For faithful Hebrews these images filled their minds with thoughts of deliverance and life. As Moses led the people they experienced the meaning of the Passover and Exodus. Under the care of Moses, God fed his people with bread-like manna in the desert. What is so startling about Jesus' remarks in this discourse is that he is not claiming to be another Moses or one more messenger in a long line of human prophets. Jesus lays claim to being the very God of Moses, the "I AM" who was and is now the companion and nourishment of God's people.

The claim of Jesus to this most holy of titles is summed up in his assertions, "It is my Father who gives you the real heavenly bread," and "I am the bread of life" (John 6:32, 48). The use of the words "I AM" is a reflection of the sacred name of Yahweh given to Moses as a revelation of the divine presence (see Exod 3:14). What Jesus is saying is that he and the "I AM" are one and the same. It is not

as a prophet of Israel but as the Divine Presence that Jesus
gives bread to the multitudes. In the Gospel of John this event takes place near the
celebration of the feast of Passover. Thus in the story, when
Jesus brings calm to the waters and preaches a new wisdom
after giving a new manna to the crowds, the Exodus events
take on an even greater meaning and significance. In all of
these events, Jesus communicates calm and peace, identify-
ing their effects with his own presence, "It is I; do not be
afraid" (John 6:20). All of these events lead us to see that
Jesus is not just another prophet; he is personally invested
with the power of the God of Moses. Jesus is the great "I
AM" who makes a new covenant with his people.

Our celebration during Holy Week has evoked the same
great images of the Passover and Exodus. The key to their
understanding is the presence and power of the God of
Moses, the I AM. Now our celebration of the Easter season puts us face-to-face with the same I AM whose power
is the source of Jesus' deliverance from death and our own
new life in him. Thus in our Easter gospel the story of the
feeding of the multitude, the calming of the waters, and the
discourse on the bread of life all form one new image of
Jesus, who is now the risen Lord. A reading of John 6:1-59
will begin to make this clearer.

The Table of the Lord

In our experience of the Easter Gospel, the "I AM"
who is speaking is not the Jesus of past history but the ris-
en Lord, whose presence in our midst can be recognized and
experienced in both his Word and the gift of the bread of
life. The Church speaks of the Eucharistic celebration as
the "table of God's word and of Christ's body."[5] This table
is spread before the people of God so that we might receive
both instruction and nourishment. This twofold experience
of God's presence in Word and meal is reflected in Jesus'
discourse on the bread which brings life to the world. His
use of the sacred name "I AM" tells us that this discourse
is not just more information about God; it contains the very

mystery of God himself. Thus what Jesus says about the bread of life is not a good rabbinic interpretation of a text; it is God's interpretation of the verse, "He gave them bread from the heavens to eat" (John 6:31).[6]

All of the discourse proper (John 6:31-58) is an embellishment of the Old Testament texts referring to Yahweh's feeding his people with bread from heaven. A believing Hebrew would understand that it refers not only to earthly bread but to the word of God which gives nourishment and life. "Not by bread alone does man live, but by every word that comes from the mouth of the Lord" (Deut 8:3). This is one of the sayings from the Old Testament which Jesus used to ward off temptation. In that context it referred to a belief that the events of the Exodus were signs of God's saving care, rather than just the physical care of Israel. Thus in using the image of heavenly bread, Jesus invites us to put faith not only in the physical signs he has performed but in the saving care of the one who performed them. In giving us the bread of life, Jesus does not offer temporary nourishment; he gives us the eternal bread of his Word. It will not pass away. It will nourish and give life forever. Jesus is this bread, and in offering to share it with us, he calls us to faith in him. Jesus invites us to "come to him," "believe in him," "look upon him," "be drawn to him," "hear him," and to "learn of him." All of these verbs invite the active response of our faith (see John 6:35, 37, 40, 44, 45).

The Word of God

In the first section of this discourse, Jesus uses the image of bread for the nourishing Word and wisdom of God. Anyone who has ever been seriously involved with and committed to God has been influenced by his Word. God's Word is both a call and a comfort, a challenge and a commission. Through his Word God has always called his people to follow his lead and live in his care. The experience of the Word as a call is echoed in the simple invitation of the risen Lord, "Follow me" (John 21:19).

The Word of God is also a comfort, and the source of the comfort is God himself. "I will take you as my own people, and you shall have me as your God" (Exod 6:7). This affirmation of God's call along with his abiding presence with his people is one of the most consistent themes of all Scripture. It spans the Word of God from the beginning to the end of revelation (see Gen 17:7-8; Rev 21:3). God is and is-with-us, and his constant message is one of comfort and peace. "Do not be afraid," "Peace be with you," and best of all, "I love you." These three words thrill every human heart. They are the words that fulfill every human hunger, and they have been addressed to us by God in the person of Jesus, "As the Father has loved me, so I have loved you" (John 15:9). What greater comfort could we have than that?

Enticing and comforting as it might be, God's Word always carries with it the challenge to "go and do the same" (Luke 10:37). This punch line to the story of the Good Samaritan is the inherent challenge contained in the images God has chosen to reveal his face. God has shown us his face in Jesus. He is loving, compassionate, and forgiving. By his own word we are challenged to go and do likewise, "As the Father has sent me, so I send you" (John 20:21). This is the challenge of involvement with God. We are sent to mirror his image to others. Jesus has shown us God's face and spoken his Word to make this challenge unquestionably clear. "Love one another as I have loved you" (John 15:12).

This challenging message has been echoed since the earliest days of instruction to the followers of Christ. "Help carry one another's burdens; in that way you will fulfill the law of Christ" (Gal 6:2). "Bear with one another; forgive whatever grievances you have against one another. Forgive as the Lord has forgiven you" (Col 3:13). Of themselves these commands seem nearly impossible, but the Christian believer must never forget that we have been commissioned by Christ to do these things in his name. We have been sent to "Go and do likewise," and the word of commission is not an empty word; it is God's own word filled with the power of the person who speaks it. This word has "comissioned" us with Christ to bring life and love to others. Remember, Jesus said, "As the Father has sent me, so I send you" (John 20:21). These words are not an empty challenge; they are a commission filled with power to give life. For after he spoke these words to his disciples, Jesus breathed and said, "Receive the Holy Spirit" (John 20:22).

The Bread of Life

The focus of his discourse shifts a bit when Jesus makes the statement, "the bread I will give is my flesh, for the life of the world" (John 6:51b). With this statement the meaning of the bread shifts from the wisdom of God's Word to the bread of Jesus' flesh and blood. The clue to the shift is that the bread which Jesus offers is to be eaten. Throughout the remainder of the discourse, the verbs shift from calls to faith to commands to eat. The heavenly bread which Jesus identifies with his life-giving flesh and blood is food for eternal life. This flesh and blood is the whole person of Jesus who will be "lifted up," thereby drawing all people together and sustaining them in life. The bread Jesus promises is himself, his crucified and risen body. In offering this bread to us, Jesus offers us his life and his love. The bread Jesus gives is indeed food for thought, but it is food for body and spirit as well.

Jesus has not only given us his words to live by, he has given us his very life, his body that was crucified, his blood that was shed for us. He has given us the very loving act of his death to live by. He has made this gift of himself available in the sign of the bread blessed and broken for us. As believers we are not only called to hear the word of Jesus, we are challenged to know that in the broken bread of the Eucharistic celebration we have Jesus himself with us. As life-giving people we are symbolic beings. We communicate love and meaning through the symbols of word and touch. Jesus has given himself to us in both these ways, Word and touch. To be fully nourished as Christian believers, we need both the bread of the Word and the bread of the Eucharist. To be sustained in life, we need both to hear and to feel the touch of love.[7]

Our Table Story

Eucharist is much more than the bread of life Jesus gave to maintain his presence among us. Eucharist is the entire pattern of life Jesus intends for his followers. Eucharist is much more than liturgy; it is Christian life itself. The gestures of Jesus at table reveal not only what Jesus did with the bread he said is his body, they reveal the pattern of Jesus' interaction with the bread of our lives which make us his Body the Church.

Jesus *took the bread.* Christ has taken the bread of our lives and joined it with his own. To take something is to lay your hands on it, to claim it for your own. Christ has laid his hand on us and claimed us for himself. He did this at baptism, and he continues to do this each time we recognize and reaffirm his *call* in our lives.

Jesus *blessed the bread.* Christ has blessed us with his life. Baptism was the first moment of that blessing. Every other moment of contact with Christ is an embellishment of that blessing. They can be prayerful moments of deep recollection or moments of life-giving contact with another person of faith. In either case they are moments of knowing the presence of the person of Christ, a presence which always brings blessing and *comfort.*

Jesus *broke the bread.* Like Christ there are moments in our lives when we feel broken. These are moments of loss or illness, moments of humiliation and hurt, moments of feeling our incompleteness, moments of loneliness, rejection, and of physical or emotional pain. Yet in these fractured moments Christ is present. Like the bread of his table, our lives are in his hands. Even when life seems to be breaking apart, we should not forget the lesson of a broken loaf of bread. It cannot be broken without being firmly held in both hands. When it comes to the breaking of bread or of our lives, both hold the *challenge* of the mystery of faith.

Jesus *gave the bread.* Christ was a giving person. He gave of his time and his touch. He gave encouragement but also challenge. He gave both Word and bread to feed and nourish. He gave most fully in giving himself. He gave till there was no more to give, declaring his life and work complete with the words, "Now it is finished" (John 19:30). Then bowing his head he handed over his spirit, the same spirit he gave us when he appeared risen from the dead. In life, death, and resurrection Jesus is a giving person. He has given us an example and challenges us to do the same. "Go and do likewise," is both a challenge and a commission. It is the *commission* to live the mystery of being bread blessed and broken for others. The best response to this challenge I have yet to hear was the simple prayer of a little girl after her first communion: "Lord, make me your bread, break me up and pass me around!"

Texts for Reading

Luke 24:13-48   The meals at Emmaus and Jerusalem
John 21:1-19   "Come and eat your meal"
John 6:1-69   "The bread I will give"

Suggestions for reflection and/or discussion:

Since the first Easter, generations of Christians have come to know Jesus in his Word and the "breaking of the bread." The following two excerpts from the Second Vatican Council express our present understanding of the celebration of the Eucharist:

From the Constitution on the Sacred Liturgy

"Christ's faithful should not be present at the celebration of the Eucharist as strangers or silent spectators. They should take part in the sacred actions, aware of what they are doing; with devotion and collaboration. They come to be instructed by God's word, and nourished at the table of the Lord's body. Giving thanks to God, they offer Christ the victim, not only through the hands of the priest, but together with him they learn to offer themselves."[8]

From the Constitution on the Church

"As often as the sacrifice of the cross by which "Christ our Pasch is sacrificed" (1 Cor 5:7) is celebrated at the altar, the work of our redemption is carried out. Likewise, in the sacrament of the Eucharistic bread, the unity of believers, who form one body in Christ (cf. 1 Cor 10:17), is both expressed and brought about. We are called to this union with Christ, who is the light of the world, from whom we go forth, through whom we live, and towards whom our whole life is directed."[9]

In the light of the above quotations, reflect on and perhaps share your responses to the following questions:

1. How do I best participate in the Eucharist as an experience of the presence of the risen Lord?
2. In what ways is my life a response to the call and comfort, the challenge and commission of Christ?
3. How have I become bread blessed and broken for others?

Suggested Prayer Service

Place a whole loaf of bread on a table in the center of the group.

Song: I Am the Bread of Life[10]
               (or some other Eucharistic hymn)

Psalm 78 or 81

Reading: Acts 10:37-41

Response: Song, Gift of Finest Wheat[11]

Gospel: John 6:48-58

Pause for reflection

Action: Join hands around the table on which the loaf of bread has been placed. Recite the Lord's Prayer together.

One person takes the loaf, breaks it in half, and breaks off a piece. The two pieces are handed on. Each person takes a piece of the loaf. All eat in silence.

After a period of silence, the leader invites spontaneous petitions from the group.

The response to the petitions could be: "Lord, feed and nourish us."

Final Prayer:

Lord Jesus Christ, you are the bread come down from heaven. Nourish and feed us with your life-giving Word. Let the bread which we now break and share in your name be a sign of our willingness to give ourselves to others as you have given yourself to us. Make us bread that gives life. We ask this in your name, Lord Jesus, now and forever.

R. Amen.

Addenda:

For a group of newly baptized and their sponsors who are sharing this Easter experience together, an appropriate action for this third week would be the celebration of the Eucharist. This could be followed by a small social or a covered dish meal. Another option would be a Eucharist celebrated with the bishop at the cathedral for all the newly baptized, along with those who have accepted full communion in the Church and their sponsors. This would be a wonderful expression of new life in the diocesan family.

Notes

1. The Eucharistic Prayers.

2. For a more complete development of this idea, see George Mac-Rae, S.J., *Invitation to John* (Garden City, N.Y.: Doubleday Image Books, 1978) 90.

3. See the gospels for the third Sunday of Easter: Cycle A, Luke 24:13-35; Cycle B, Luke 24:35-48; Cycle C, John 21:1-19.

4. See the first reading for Easter Sunday, Cycles A, B, C, Acts 10:34, 37-43.

5. General Instruction of the Roman Missal #8.

6. This verse is based on texts found in Exod 16:4f; Ps 78:24.

7. For a more complete development of this thought, see Michael J. Taylor, S.J., *John, the Different Gospel.* (Staten Island, N.Y.: Alba House, 1983) 69-70.

8. See Flannery, Constitution on the Sacred Liturgy #48, 16–17.

9. See Flannery, Constitution on the Church #3, 351.

10. See *Songs of Praise,* Vol. I, #36.

11. *People's Mass Book* (new edition) #665.

Chapter 4

Jesus Expands the Image
The Fourth Week of Easter

This fourth week of the Easter season marks the mid-point of our celebration of faith. This week is unique for many reasons. The readings of the Lectionary selected for our reflection do not form a continuous whole. They are a series of short discourses which evoke images of who Jesus is for the Church. These word pictures expand our own image of Jesus and lead us into the mystery of his care and concern for the flock. They expand our horizons, leading us beyond our earthly images to the glorious image of a Jesus who is one with the God he calls "Father."

Faith and Imagery

Just as the Second Vatican Council has drawn upon the rich imagery presented in the Scriptures to develop a better sense of the Church, we can draw upon the images that Jesus has given to develop a better outlook on who he is for us. One of the great challenges of faith in any age is the development of a healthy image of God. The word pictures Jesus gives us in this Easter season can help us to do just that.

As we begin our reflections, it is good to remember that these images are not of our making; they are given to us by Christ himself. They are the images of the gate and the shepherd, and the image of Jesus as the way, truth, and life. These word pictures are Jesus' way of showing us what God is like. He said it himself, "Whoever has seen me has seen the Father" (John 14:9). Through these images Jesus has begun to reveal the glory of God. No wonder then that the Church has made them a part of the Easter Gospel; for Easter is not only a feast of new life for us, it is a feast of God's glory.

This week also marks a transition in our reading of the Gospel of John. As we reflect on the images that Jesus has given us both to describe himself and to reveal the Father, we pass from the first part of the Gospel called The Book of Signs to the second part called the Book of Glory. In our celebration of the Easter season thus far we have witnessed the signs of Jesus' resurrection appearances. We have also recalled the sign of Cana, the giving of sight to the man born blind, and the raising of Lazarus. Last week we experienced the feeding of the multitudes. All of these "signs" have led us to a deeper understanding of the life and ministry of Jesus. Now we move even deeper into the meaning of who Jesus is, his inner life and destiny. Through a series of images, we will move from signs for this world to the glory of God, a glory Jesus says he had before the world began (see John 17:5).

Jesus, Sheepgate and Shepherd

> I am the good shepherd, says the Lord; I know my sheep and mine know me, alleluia!
>
> *Gospel Acclamation*
> *Monday of the Fourth Week of Easter*

It would be appropriate at this point to read John 10:1-18, 22-30.

One of the most universally reverenced images of Jesus is that of the Good Shepherd. It is an image that says so much, and yet its meaning is never exhausted. It is an appealing image, and yet it is not without its challenge. The Good Shepherd will provide access to the pastures of divine life, yet we must listen for and respond to his voice. The Good Shepherd is a comforting image, but it is also one of challenge and call.

It is the voice of the risen Lord who says "I am the sheepgate" (John 10:7). "I am the good shepherd" (John 10:11). By laying down his life, Jesus has become the source of life for others. That was why he came. By his death and resurrection Jesus has opened the pathways to life, the same eternal life he shares with the Father. Jesus is the gate to this life, and he provides access to it. He not only provides an entry, he is the Way itself. "I am the gate. Whoever enters through me will be safe. They will go in and out, and find pasture" (John 10:9). Jesus provides access to the pastures of life in God. He himself is the means of access and familiarity in our relationship with God. Through his death and resurrection Jesus has heard and responded to the cry of God's people, "Open to me the gates of justice" (Ps 118:19). He has not only opened the gate, Jesus declares that he is the gate. No wonder then we have the song of Easter praise, "This gate is the Lord's; the just shall enter it" (Ps 118:20). In Christ no one can rob us of life. In him we are safe and secure and have found the fullness of life he came to bring. In Christ we have entered the gates of justice and can give thanks to the Lord.

"I lay down my life—I take it up again"

The Easter season provides all believers an opportunity to sing a song of praise to God for the life so generously shared with us. It is a time of joy and a time of celebrating faith in the Good Shepherd who has laid down his life for the sheep. Jesus is that Good Shepherd who has not only sacrificed himself for the sake of the flock but who has established a deep personal bond with each of his sheep. "I know my sheep and my sheep know me" (John 10:14). Not only has Jesus laid down his life for the flock, but in taking it up again through resurrection, Jesus now offers a special life of intimate union with himself to all those who hear his voice and follow him.

The voice of Jesus the eternal shepherd is the voice of the I AM who led the first members of the flock from slavery to freedom in the land of promise. In Jesus we now have access to that same freedom and promise. "My sheep hear my voice. I know them, and they follow me. I give them eternal life" (John 10:27-28). To be a disciple is to follow Jesus. In following our good shepherd, we find pasture and life. Jesus is that life, a life that is full and marked with the eternal quality of God himself. In the resurrection of Jesus, believers see that their shepherd transcends human death and lives on to be an eternal shepherd who tends his sheep forever.

"The Lord is my shepherd"

The image of Jesus as Good Shepherd unites so many ways of viewing him. Jesus has and shares eternal life. He nourishes and feeds his flock. He will search out and return lost sheep to the flock. He wants to establish and sustain a personal relationship with each of his sheep. The Scriptures abound with images of the shepherd. Psalm 23 declares, "The Lord is my shepherd" (Ps 23:1), and in the prophet Ezekiel the Lord speaks out against the shepherds of Israel who have neglected the flock, declaring in solemn promise, "I myself will look after and tend my sheep" (Ezek 34:11). In the Gospels Jesus speaks of seeking out a single lost sheep; not even one stray is beyond his effort or his love (see Matt 18:12-14; Luke 15:4-9).

In the Gospel of John, the shepherd imagery is the most vivid of all. Jesus embodies the guidance, care, and companionship God offers not only to his people but to individuals. In this shepherd discourse of our Easter Gospel, Jesus describes the mutuality of the relationship he enjoys with each of his disciples. He leads out and goes before his sheep. He also calls them by name, establishing a personal bond with each one by extending a personal invitation to follow him. Thus in Jesus believers can truly pray, "The Lord is my shepherd" (Ps 23:1).

One Flock—One Shepherd

The work of Jesus as shepherd is to gather and unite all his sheep into one flock. The word flock is a good image to describe the many types of believers, loyal or wandering, and the many levels of belief, devoted or confused. As a good shepherd Jesus does not force his role as shepherd on anyone; he simply calls and invites us into his care and his flock. This can be freely chosen or freely rejected. When accepted there is cause for great rejoicing, for it is then we know the personal love Jesus has for us, his sheep. It is in the personal relationship Jesus shares with us as our shepherd that we learn the lesson of self-acceptance; for in calling and caring for us, Jesus acknowledges our true identity. In giving us the title, "my sheep," Jesus calls us with the gospel word for repentant believers.[1] It is for us and for our salvation that he has come and given his life. Thus as Good Shepherd Jesus both provides the way to life and shares life itself with those who come to him. The life Jesus offers comes to us as living water, heavenly bread, and light and life from above.[2] In offering these gifts, Jesus offers his gentle life-giving care as a shepherd. To accept and to follow is up to us.

Jesus' Hour of Glory

Shortly after the last and great sign of the raising of Lazarus, Jesus announced, "The hour has come for the Son of Man to be glorified" (John 12:23). With this announcement the mood of John's Gospel changes. At this point the audience to whom Jesus speaks takes on a new focus. In the Book of Signs the words and deeds of Jesus were for all to see and hear. Now Jesus begins to address only his disciples, who despite their imperfect faith still follow him. Thus the second half of John's Gospel, The Book of Glory, is a book for believers. Only believers can understand the hour of Jesus, because only they accept him as the one sent by the Father to reveal and share his life, light, and love.

The Book of Glory is the unfolding of that love story and an invitation to share Jesus' light and life.

The Book of Glory has four major sections. It begins with the account of the Last Supper and a detailed description of Jesus' washing of his disciples' feet (see John 13:1-38). In this inaugural scene the focus of Jesus' ministry shifts to those who believe in him. It is to those who believe that Jesus shares the secrets of his heart. The next section forms the group of passages selected as our Easter Gospel for the remaining weeks of the season. They are a collection of discourses given by Jesus at the table of the Last Supper (see John 14:1-17:26). This whole sequence is an original feature of the Gospel of John. The Church is correct in putting these discourses before the faithful during the Easter season, after our celebration of the events of Good Friday and Easter. These "farewell discourses," as they are called, are a commentary in anticipation on the narratives of the passion and resurrection. What better time to reflect upon them than after our celebration of the events upon which Jesus has shared his thoughts? His words will bring a new depth and richness to the mystery.

The final two sections of the Book of Glory are the passion narrative and the resurrection narrative (see John 18:1—19:42; 20:1-29). It is these two sections that form the heart of the Church's reflection on and celebration of Jesus' hour of glory. For believers this mystery of Christ's dying and rising is the core of our faith. It is always from the vantage point of the Christ who has died and is risen that we enter into reflection and share a celebration of our faith in the Lord. That is what makes the Easter season an ideal time for renewal of faith in Jesus, who is always our way, our truth, and our life.

Jesus, The Way, Truth and Life

> I am the Way, the Truth, and the Life says the Lord; no one comes to the Father, except through me. Alleluia!
>
> *Gospel Acclamation*
> *Friday of the Fourth Week of Easter*

At this point it would be a good idea to read John 14:1-14. In a second reflection for this Easter week we find ourselves at table with Jesus listening, along with the disciples, to his final discourse. In it Jesus tells us he is going away. Unlike the first disciples our hearts are not troubled; they are full of joy. We know the place to which Jesus has gone. As we continue to celebrate our Easter faith, Jesus' announcement about the "many dwelling places" in his Father's house is a reason for renewed joy. Because of his resurrection Jesus is not absent, he is with the Father and invites us to join him in that union of life and love.

The departure of Jesus was a victorious passing over to the Father in glory. Now Jesus calls us to follow him in a life of union with God. The images Jesus uses of "place," "many dwellings," and "Father's house" are not so much pictures of heaven as they are signs and metaphors for the "area" of communion with God. In many ways they refer to Jesus himself, who is the new and eternal place for meeting and communing with God. Jesus is the new and indestructible temple, the place where believers worship God in spirit and truth. In this discourse the Easter Gospel goes to great lengths to make it clear that the process of dwelling with God begins long before heaven; it begins with our sharing the light, life, and love of Jesus here and now.

Light Along the Way

Sometimes it seems that followers of Christ interpret the Christian message so it sounds like this: "There's light at the end of the tunnel." Now to someone who is lost that may be good news, but it is not the Christian Gospel. The message of Christ is that "there is light in the midst of darkness." Jesus, the risen Lord, is the light we follow. Though our vision is blurred and faulty at times, we know the way. We have no need to say to Jesus, "Show us." Our faith and our experience of Jesus have shown us he is the Way, the Truth, and the Life. All of the "signs" point to it. There is no new way to be revealed; Jesus is it.

The words and deeds of Jesus communicate truth and life. They are the hearable and seeable revelation of the

Father. Jesus said, "If you really knew me, you would know my Father also" (John 14:7), and "Whoever has seen me has seen the Father" (John 14:9). These statements are some of the strongest assertions in all the good news that Jesus is the revelation of God himself. Jesus is the image of the Father. The more we know of him, the more we know of God. If we hear Jesus we hear the Father; if we see Jesus we see the Father.

Jesus is a sharer as well as a revealer. He is the way to truth. He is the way to life. Jesus declared this when he said he was a gate, an entryway to God's abundant life (see John 10:9-10). The image of the way is another means Jesus employs to express the reality of communion with himself and with the Father. It is an Exodus image, an image of journey. Through his resurrection Jesus has gone before us to seek out a place for us and lead us to it. That place is a new land of promise, the land of our new and life-giving relationship with God. The promise of that land is not in some far-off heaven; it is our life here and now, our present journey in faith. We know the way and walk upon it, for the ground of that land is Jesus.

Jesus calls us to walk where he walks, to dwell where he dwells. He tells us that where he is there are many dwelling places, there is ample room for all. Jesus' life and love is so immense that the dwelling places in it are limitless. In Jesus believers have found both truth and life; we have come to see and hear the love of God made flesh. In Jesus we have found the way.

These images are a challenge for us to review what we have seen and heard up to now. Our Lenten observance, the celebration of the paschal mystery, and our renewal in faith all help us to see and hear Jesus more clearly. We have a better image of who he is for us. Our reflections on the Book of Signs have revealed Jesus as our light and our life. He is the very love of God made flesh. Now in the Book of Glory we begin to see the Jesus who is lifted up forever. In this Jesus we will see the face of God and live.

Texts for Reading

John 10:1-18	I am the Good Shepherd
John 12:44-50	I have come as light
John 14:1-14	I am the way, truth, and life

Suggestions for reflection and/or discussion:

Jesus has come to reflect the image of the Father. As Good Shepherd, Light for the world, and in the images of way, truth, and life, Jesus reveals the father's face.

1. What image do I have of God? A better way to ask this question is, when someone says, "Think of God," what word or picture comes to mind?
2. Are the Scriptural pictures that Jesus gives to show who God is part of my faith imagery?
3. How do I respond to Jesus' question, "Who do you say that I am?"

Suggested Prayer Service

Opening Song: I Am the Way[4]
                       Shepherd's Alleluia[5]
                       Psalm of the Good Shepherd[6]
Pause for silent prayer

Psalm 23 (if not sung as the opening song) or Psalm 84

Reading: Ezekiel 34:1-16

After, or in place of the reading, someone may want to recount the following story.

A Shepherd's Story

Many years ago in a little Irish village, some women brought a young orphan boy to the local parish priest. They asked him to take the growing lad into his care. The priest took the boy, provided food and lodging, and with the help of his people provided the boy with money for an education. About the time the lad was to graduate from secondary school, the priest asked him what he would like to be in life. "Oh, Father, I would like to be an actor and study the plays of Shakespeare."

Again with the help of his parishioners, the priest provided the young man with enough money to go across the sea and begin his studies. The boy worked, studied hard, and distinguished himself as a budding young actor. Upon graduation he joined an acting troupe and began to play the parts he knew so well—Lear, Macbeth, and Othello. His career developed, and he toured the Continent. He even went to America.

Once when in Dublin, he made a point to return to the little village of his childhood and to visit his friend, the now very old priest. The priest was delighted to see him and planned a little reception for him after Mass the next Sunday. At the reception all marveled at his fine appearance and his way with words. They asked him to recite from the great plays of Shakespeare, and before their eyes the wonderful characters came to life. At the end of the morning, the people asked the young actor to do one more thing. "Read Psalm twenty-three to us," they asked. "I will on one condition," the young man said, looking at his old friend the priest, "that Father does it too." With that the old man nodded.

So with Bible in hand, the actor recited the words we know so well, "The Lord is my shepherd . . . ." All were attentive, and when he finished there was a quiet hush. Then he motioned to the old priest, who with the help of his cane walked to the center of the group. Then with eyes closed and head bowed he began to recite the psalm by heart. His words were moving and prayerful. He spoke of the shepherd who had called and led him through life; how he had anointed him, guided him through times of darkness, and provided food at the table; how goodness followed him always and how his hope was to dwell in the Lord's house forever. When he completed the prayer all were still; a reverent awe filled the room. As the old man returned to his seat, the actor got up to thank the people for the wonderful day. "Thank you," he said, "you have been most kind, but I want you to remember one thing." Then turning to the old priest, the young man said, "With my skill, I can do many things. But," and placing his hand on the old man's shoulder, he said, "Remember this, he knows the good shepherd."

Pause for reflection and possible sharing on your favorite image of the Lord.

All recite the Lord's Prayer

Concluding Prayer:

God and Father of our Lord Jesus Christ, you have sent your son to reveal your face. Help us to follow Jesus, our shepherd. Keep our ears open to the sound of his voice and lead our steps in the way he has shown. We ask this through Christ our Lord. Amen.

Notes

1. Sheep is a Gospel word for a repentant believer. See Matt 18:12-14; Luke 15:4-7. See also Taylor, p. 119, for the use of the word in John 10:10, 14-15.

2. These images are presented to us both in the sequence of the Gospel of John and in the readings from the Lectionary as the principal images for the Lenten and Easter season's sacramental catechesis. See John 4:14 and 7:38; John 6:35; John 8:12 and 9:5; John 11:25.

3. These images are found earlier in the Gospel of John. See John 2:19; 4:21-24.

4. See *People's Mass Book* (New Edition) #102.

5. See *Glory and Praise,* Vol. 2, #138 (Phoenix, Ariz.: North American Liturgy Resources).

6. See *Glory and Praise,* Vol. 3, #231.

Chapter 5

Discipleship and Service
The Fifth Week of Easter

Live in me and let me live in you, says the Lord;
my branches bear much fruit. Alleluia!
Gospel Acclamation
Wednesday of the Fifth Week of Easter

In this acclamation for the Easter Gospel, the Church proclaims faith in the risen Lord as the source of our life and fruitfulness. This acclamation, made up from two verses of Scripture, John 15:4-5, is an example of the praying Church exercising its role as interpreter and communicator of the mission and message of Christ. Christ is the center and heart of the life of faith, and the liturgical texts continually encourage our celebration of the various aspects of his centrality in our lives. The seasons of the liturgical year and the Scriptural readings that accompany them are the sources not only of our catechesis in Christ but of our celebration of his presence in our midst. Thus the celebration of the Easter season and its Gospel are both an impetus to our development in faith and a renewing experience of the risen Lord himself.[1]

This week in our Easter experience we celebrate both our union with Christ in discipleship and our life-giving fruitfulness in him through ministry to others. These aspects of our faith-life in Christ are presented in the discourse on the vine and the branches and in the gesture of Christ washing the feet of his disciples. These two images can help us in a reflection on the meaning of discipleship and the challenge of Christian service. Both these images show something about our union with Christ and the fruitfulness that comes from that union. The images of the vine and the branches and the footwashing are verbal pictures of our call to discipleship and the challenge of Christ's commandment of love.

Love, the Key to Glory

In the Gospel of John, the Book of Glory begins with a solemn opening scene that sets the stage for all that will follow (see John 13:1-35). Jesus is seated with his disciples at the table of the Last Supper. It is "the hour" for him to pass from this world to his Father. Having loved his own in this world, he is about to show them his love to the end. This loving attitude of the heart of Jesus is something he will manifest in both word and deed. Jesus called his disciples to be "his own" and to share a life of unity with him. Now he is about to dramatize and discourse on the meaning of that life and that call. For Jesus there is only one meaning; the call to life in him is the sharing of a bond of love. That is what is meant by glory.

In popular terms love is often thought of as an emotional attachment. Jesus' love is much more constant and profound than that. His love is one of total commitment, a love of total surrender and service. It is a love that Jesus desires to be reflected in the lives of his disciples. For the followers of Jesus, loving service of others is the "sign" of the union between Christ and each disciple. Thus it is in the keeping of "the commandment" that the mystery of union with Christ comes to fruition. Christ's commandment is, of course, "Love one another as I have loved you" (John 15:12). His love is a love of faithful self-surrender. It is a love that we can only hope to achieve by continually growing in our union with him. In the discourse on the vine and the branches, Jesus explains the meaning of our union with him and the effects this love-bond has for others.

"I am the vine"

The imagery of the vine is common in Old Testament writings for the people of God. They were planted by God. They were his vineyard. "He spaded it, cleared it of stones, and planted the choicest vines" (Isa 5:2). Then he waited for a crop of fine choice grapes. What came forth was wild and untended. Instead of the fruits of justice, bloodshed and disunity blossomed (see Isa 5:4, 7). What a disappointment Israel was to the Lord after all the loving care he lavished upon it! "In a fertile field by plentiful waters it was planted, to grow branches, bear fruit, and become a majestic vine" (Ezek 17:8). Despite its infidelity Israel knew its origins, its special place in the heart of God. No wonder the psalmist cries out, prayerfully recalling Israel's history, while begging the Lord to lavish his loving care on it once again. "A vine from Egypt you transplanted . . . it took root and filled the land . . . Once again, O Lord of hosts, look down from heaven, and see; Take care of this vine, and protect what your right hand has planted" (Ps 80:9, 10, 15).

The vineyard imagery of the Old Testament is rich and colorful, evoking thoughts of abundant harvests and good luscious fruit. For the true Israelite, fruitfulness was bound up with justice and love. To bear fruit was to keep the commandments of the Lord with emphasis on acting justly and loving tenderly. Often the fruit Israel produced lacked the qualities the Lord desired. It is only in the New Testament and in Jesus that we find the fruition of the just and tender qualities of God's love. Jesus is the true vine planted in the house of the Lord. It is only from him that the fruit of mutual love will blossom.

At this point a reading of John 15:1-17 would be helpful. This section is part of the farewell discourses in John's Gospel. Through these discourses Jesus prepared his disciples for his departure by reflecting on the meaning of the life and love he so freely shared with them. Here the Scriptural imagery of the vine is applied to Jesus in a personal way. Reading them after the events of Holy Week, we can see the full implications of the imagery Jesus evokes by saying, "I am the true vine" (John 15:1). Jesus is the true Israelite who is the beloved of the Father. It is as the vine that he speaks of laying down his life. "There is no greater love than this:" Jesus says, "to lay down one's life for one's friends" (John 15:13). In self-sacrifice Jesus, the heavenly vine, has laid down his life for us. He is the true vine trimmed clean by his vinedresser Father so that he might produce more abundant fruit. He has borne this fruit in love, love until death. As risen Lord Jesus, the life-giving vine, now shares the fruit of his labors with all who are united with him, so that together they might produce an abundant harvest of justice and love. The risen Jesus is the majestic vine planted by God in the fertile field of this world. Because he is raised up in glory, he can now grow more branches and bear even more abundant fruit.

"You are the branches"

This image of Jesus' union with his disciples is part of the Easter Gospel, because only the risen Christ can proclaim the full meaning of the image of the vine and the branches. It is as the risen "I AM" that Jesus most fully embodies the message of our union in him. It is the risen Lord who is alive and in our midst, and he is known and recognized by the vitality of his branches. Jesus is not just the stalk, he is the whole vine. Thus as branches we are in union with him and share in his life (see John 15:5).

However, just as Jesus was cleansed and pruned, those joined to him must also know the cleansing of God's Word and the pruning of his love. We are cleansed, Jesus says, thanks to the Word he has spoken to us. How attentive we need to be to God's Word if it is to have its cleansing effect in our lives! How sensitive we need to become to the pruning effects of his love! This cleansing and pruning is the work of the vinedresser Father within us to increase our life of union with Jesus, the real vine. "He who lives in me and I in him, will produce abundantly" (John 15:5b). We live and love in Jesus because through his resurrection the vine the Father has planted now has branches. Thus during the Easter season the newly baptized remind all the faithful of the vitality and fruitfulness we share in our common discipleship in Christ. Together we are called to glorify the Father with Jesus by showing forth the fruit of his love in our lives. By sharing one life we also share one love. Together we live in his love, thus bringing forth the fruit of discipleship. This can only be done through constant prayer, asking for an increase of growth in the Christian life, and through mutual help and example from those already deeply united to Christ. As the Father chose Israel, Jesus has chosen us, "to go forth and bear fruit" (John 15:16). Just as the Father has been glorified in the mission of his son, now the Father is glorified in the continuation of that mission by the son's disciples, the risen sons and daughters who share Christ's life through baptism (see John 15:8; Rom 6:4).

"Live on in my love"

Throughout the discourse on the vine and the branches, Jesus clearly tells us to live in his love. We do this if we keep his commandment, namely to share his love with others, just as he has shared it with us. It may sound trite, but it is true: love is not love until you give it away. It is in the sharing of Jesus' love that we find and give witness to his life. That is the secret of Jesus' risen joy and that is what he shares with us. "All this I tell you that my joy may be yours and your joy may be complete. This is my commandment: love one another as I have loved you" (John 15:11-12). While it is true that Jesus' love brought him to the point of self-sacrifice, as Easter believers we must never forget that his loving gift of self did not end in death but blossomed into new life. Any suffering involved in loving as Jesus loves is never the kind of suffering that brings about death. It is a self-sacrificing pain, like that of a woman in labor; it is a sacrifice that brings forth new life. The disciple who lives and loves in Jesus not only shares in his self-sacrifice; resurrection is part of the experience too. Thus together with Jesus we share life, love, and joy. In him we are all beloved disciples, cleansed and made one by the love of his Word and the waters of baptism (see John 15:3; 13:7, 10).

"I give you an example"

The word of Jesus makes us clean. This is his own teaching. But Jesus never taught by words alone; he taught also by example. Thus at the same table where Jesus taught about union of life in him, he dramatized the challenge of this union he called discipleship by giving an example of loving service to others. Union of life in Christ the vine is to be evidenced by bearing the fruit of love. Jesus embodied this teaching when he linked his commandment of love to a vivid lesson in service, the washing of the disciples' feet. This dramatic gesture shows the spirit of Jesus' self-giving on behalf of his disciples. Through word and deed Jesus shows the greatness of his love. Thus in the discourse on loving as Jesus has loved us, we see spelled out in words what we know Jesus has acted out in the flesh. He has become our servant.

Here it is appropriate to read the footwashing story, John 13:1-17. This is the Gospel for the evening Eucharist celebrated on Holy Thursday. It serves as a reminder that we have been cleansed by the Lord's death and resurrection and commissioned to be servants of his life and love for others. While there are overtones of baptism in the gesture, it is the lesson in service and the power of self-sacrifice behind that service that seem to demand most attention. Jesus himself said that his disciples would not fully understand the meaning of this gesture (see John 13:7). Only after the resurrection did his followers understand the meaning of this word and deed; for only then did they experience the cleansing action and commissioning spirit of his self-sacrificing and life-giving love.[2]

"That you may believe"

Before Jesus asked us to become life-giving servants like himself, he first knelt before us and asked that we allow him to serve us, to love us. Jesus has washed us into his loving death and resurrection, into a life which he has put aside and taken up again. When Jesus began the foot-washing of his disciples, he first took off his cloak and then picked up the towel and basin (see John 13:4-5). The word describing Jesus' action is the same word used in the shepherd image to describe his loving action of "laying down" or "putting aside" his life for us (see John 10:17-18). When Jesus finished washing the disciples' feet, he "put his cloak back on" (John 13:12) to join his disciples once more at table. Again the word describing his action is the same one used to speak of the shepherd's power "to take up" his life again. It was in the laying down and taking up of life that Jesus experienced the Father's love as never before. It was in this action that he fulfilled the command he received from his Father. It was "for this," Jesus said, "the Father loves me" (John 10:17). Thus when Jesus commanded his disciples to "wash each other's feet" (John 13:14), he not only gave them a new commandment, he pledged to them a share in his dying and rising, a share in his Father's life-sustaining and everlasting love.

Through the washing of the feet, Jesus not only gave us an example, he became an exemplar of the life-sustaining power of the Father's love, a love that sustained him through the cleansing action of his death and resurrection. Through this word and deed Jesus gave one dramatic illustration of his teaching on discipleship: "As the Father has loved me, so I have loved you. Live on in my love" (John 15:9), and "I tell you this now, before it takes place, so that when it takes place you may believe that I AM" (John 13:19).

"Wash each other's feet"

Jesus loves us as he has been loved. The challenge of that comfort is that now we are to go and do the same (see John 15:9; 13:34). No wonder at the end of the supper and the footwashing, Jesus said, "Now is the Son of Man glorified and God is glorified in him" (John 13:31). Jesus was proclaiming that believers would be recognized as his disciples by the sign of their love for one another (see John 13:35). Discipleship is not just abiding in Jesus; it is loving one another as he has loved us. It is in service to others that the branches on the vine bear fruit. Like the branches and the vine themselves, the commandment of love and the washing of the feet are intertwined. Disciples not only share Jesus' "heritage" in the life that comes through his death and resurrection, they are challenged to imitate the spirit behind that life-giving action (John 13:8). Discipleship is the bearing forth of the fruit of love, a making visible of the invisible presence of the glorified Lord (see John 15:8). It is the risen Christ who has loved us and washed us clean. It is his life-giving spirit that empowers us to love one another as he has loved us. Some Christian Churches consider the footwashing action a "sacrament." This is certainly true in the wide sense of the word; it is a "sign" of the Lord's commandment of love. But we must not overlook an even greater "sign," that of the baptized footwashers. Through our own loving fulfillment of Christ's commandment we become recognized for who we are, living branches, true disciples, and "signs," life-giving "sacraments" of the glorified Lord himself.

Beloved Disciples

Before we move on from the scene of the table and the footwashing, there is an unnamed yet important disciple we should meet. He is known only by the phrase, "the disciple whom Jesus loved" (John 13:23). No doubt this figure is an individual disciple for whom Jesus has a special fondness. But his appearance in the Gospel of John is not only because of who he is, but how he embodies the true image of Christian discipleship. He is the "beloved disciple" because he knows how to love as Jesus loves.

The figure of the beloved disciple is introduced at the table of the Last Supper and has a prominent role to play in the rest of John's Gospel. This disciple is pictured as someone who has a privileged relationship with Jesus. He reclines next to the Lord at the supper and leans "back against Jesus' chest" to engage in private conversation (John 13:25). This same posture and sense of intimacy is used in the beginning of John's Gospel to describe Jesus' own relationship with his Father. Jesus is pictured as "ever at the Father's side," and because of this posture and the intimate conversation it fosters, Jesus can reveal the Father (John 1:18). So too with the beloved disciple. If anyone knows the meaning of Jesus and his love, it is this disciple. He enjoys a special relationship with Jesus and knows the secrets of his heart. He embodies the commandment to love as Jesus loves.

The beloved disciple is, however, no dreamer swooning at the side of Jesus. He is a true disciple, a friend of the Lord, and a friend of the other disciples. He never stands alone in any of the scenes where he appears in the Gospel. He is always in relationship with other disciples, sharing life, giving support, showing compassion, and prompting faith. At the supper he communicates with Peter and the Lord, at the cross he stands in solidarity with Mary, at the tomb he responds to the Magdalene's story and accompanies Peter in a quest for faith.[3]

This disciple stands by the others because he has stood by his Lord. From what he has learned and experienced at the side of Jesus, he had the courage to stand by his Lord in time of trial and persecution, even death. Whatever he learned from his union with Christ, it sustained him so that even in the face of the empty tomb, he believed.[4] Both faith and love have a secure home in this disciple's heart. His discipleship is a model for ours; his bond with Christ and the other disciples is an example to all of us. The beloved disciple shows us how to fulfill the commandment of love, how to be a branch that bears good fruit.

Texts for Reading

John 15:1-8   Vine and Branches
John 15:9-17   Friends and Lovers

Suggestions for reflection and/or discussion:

Jesus, the vine, shares his life with each branch. He shares his life and love as a humble, faithful servant and wants us to do the same.

1. Does my own personal friendship with Jesus help me in the learning process of sharing his love with others?
2. How does my own call to discipleship image the dying and rising of Jesus?
3. Could I single out something I do, or the way I do it, and say, "That's my ministry?"

Suggested Prayer Service

Opening Song: I Am the Vine[5]
                          Where Charity and Love Prevail[6]
                          The Lord Jesus[7]

Prayer:

Lord Jesus Christ, you are the vine; we are the branches. Keep us always attentive to your Word and united in love with our brothers and sisters. Help us to love one another as you have loved us. We ask this through Christ our Lord. Amen.

Reading: Colossians 3:12-17 or Luke 7:43-47a

Pause for reflection

Optional Action: There could be a service of the washing of one another's feet. Let a leader begin and then each one in turn wash the feet of the person next to them. Some recorded background music would add a reflective atmosphere to this prayerful activity.

Litany of the "I Am's"

Lord, you said, "I am the bread of life" (John 6:48). Nourish us always with your Word and Eucharist.

R. Lord, hear our prayer.

Lord, you said, "I am the light of the world" (John 9:5). Shine in our hearts as a beacon of truth.

R. Lord, hear our prayer.

Lord, you said, "I am the sheepgate" (John 10:7). Open to us and show us the way.

R. Lord, hear our prayer.

Lord, you said, "I am the good shepherd" (John 10:11). Call us into the pastures of your everlasting life.

R. Lord, hear our prayer.

Lord, you said, "I am the resurrection and the life" (John 11:25). Remove from our hearts the tombstone of sin.

R. Lord, hear our prayer.

Lord, you said, "I am the way, and the truth, and the life" (John 14:6). Lead us always to your Father's kingdom.

R. Lord, hear our prayer.

Lord, you said, "I am the true vine" (John 15:1). Help us to bring forth the good fruits of your love.

R. Lord, hear our prayer.

The Lord's Prayer

Prayer of Blessing and Dismissal:

Loving Father, help our brothers and sisters to grow in the knowledge of the Gospel of the risen Christ. May they love you and their neighbor with a generous heart and a willing spirit. Let them grow in a life of holiness and count them always among the members of your Church. We ask this through Jesus Christ, our Lord. Amen.[8]

Notes

1. The Church has always seen the seasons and texts of our liturgical celebrations as a source for the nourishment and growth of faith. Archbishop Virgilio Noe gave a reminder of this in an address at Catholic University. He said, "In the celebration of the liturgy the church confesses her faith; the liturgy is the living voice of tradition . . . the teaching given in the liturgy is more accessible to the faithful than a course of study; the liturgical books are the church's theological books" (cited in *Origins,* 14, no. 8 [July 13, 1984]).

2. Most scholars see the footwashing as a prophetic action representing the death of Jesus. It expresses in symbol the love by which Jesus undertook the most lowly service of all in order to bring life and refreshment to others. See Taylor, 156-157, McRae, 169-170.

3. For a series of texts on the Beloved Disciple see John 13:24; 19:26; 20:1-10.

4. The courage and loyalty of the Beloved Disciple are indicated in John 18:5; 19:26; 20:8. Several scholars have written on the Beloved Disciple in recent years. A brief yet good account of recent findings is summarized in Sr. Rea McDonnell, SSND, "Discipleship in the Johannine Community," *New Catholic World* 225 (Jan-Feb, 1983) 24-27.

5. *People's Mass Book* (New Edition) #104.

6. *Ibid.* #659.

7. *Glory and Praise,* Vol. 3 #264.

8. Model prayers of blessing can be found in the RCIA #121-124, and #374. They could be modified for blessing the faithful during the Easter season.

Chapter 6

The Promise of the Spirit-Paraclete
The Sixth Week of Easter

> Believe me, it is for your own good that I am going. If I do
> not go, the Paraclete will not come. Alleluia!
>
> *Antiphon for Mary's Canticle*
> *Tuesday of the Sixth Week of Easter*

One of the secrets of the heart of Jesus that he shares
so freely with his disciples is that it is better for us that he
has gone away. It was only by Jesus' going that the Spirit
has come. That is why Jesus began his farewell discourse
with the words "Do not let your hearts be troubled. Have
faith in God and faith in me" (John 14:1). Jesus prepared
his disciples for the pain of his suffering, but he also raised
their hopes with the promise of his Spirit. "I will ask the
Father and he will give you another Paraclete—to be with
you always: the Spirit of truth" (John 14:16-17a). "I tell
you the sober truth: It is much better for you that I go. If
I fail to go, the Paraclete will never come to you, whereas
if I go, I will send him to you" (John 16:7). The Spirit is

a gift of both the Father and Jesus. Jesus can send the Spirit because he has gone to the Father. The Father sends the Spirit because Jesus has asked him to share his love for those who love him (see John 14:23). The Father already loves us, Jesus says, because we have believed that he came from God. "I did indeed come from the Father," Jesus said, "I came into the world. Now I am leaving the world to go to the Father" (John 16:28). Jesus has spoken quite plainly. He linked his going away to the Father with the coming of the Holy Spirit.

Ascension-Pentecost

The going of Jesus and the coming of the Spirit are part of the Easter mystery. We have seen this already in the Easter Gospel. Jesus announced his ascension to the Magdalene and commissioned her to proclaim the good news to the other disciples, "I am ascending to my Father and your Father, to my God and your God" (John 20:17).[1] On the evening of that same first day, Jesus joined the disciples in the upper room where he had bid his farewell and said, "Peace be with you. . . . As the Father has sent me, so I send you" (John 20:21). Then in a gesture which was reminiscent of the first creation, he breathed on them and said, "Receive the Holy Spirit" (John 20:22).[2] The Church celebrates these two mysteries of the going of Jesus to the Father and his giving of the Holy Spirit in the feasts of Ascension and Pentecost. We celebrate them not only as events in the life of Christ but also as events in the life of the Church, since they are linked with Jesus' commission of the disciples to be his witnesses.

The Ascension-Pentecost event is the fulfillment of the Easter experience. Through the risen Lord Christians are empowered and commissioned with his Spirit to be witnesses to his resurrection. With joy and exultation the Church celebrates this mystery in an "unending hymn of praise." "Father, all powerful and ever-living God, we do well always and everywhere to give you thanks through Jesus Christ our Lord. In his risen body he plainly showed himself to his disciples and was taken up to heaven in their sight to claim for us a share in his divine life.'''[3] "Father, you sent the Holy Spirit on those marked out to be your children by sharing the life of your only Son, and so you brought the paschal mystery to its completion.''[4] The unity of this mystery is celebrated in one "triumphant song": "He ascended above all the heavens, and from his throne at your right hand poured into the hearts of your adopted children the Holy Spirit of your promise.''[5] The sending of the Holy Spirit is the crowning gift of the Easter mystery. Our baptismal commission to be witnesses to Jesus is the inaugural grace of the Easter experience. Easter-Ascension-Pentecost are one feast, one mystery; they are not an ending, they are a new beginning. That is why Jesus clearly told his disciples, "It is much better for you that I go" (John 16:7).

"Eyes to see, ears to hear"

Jesus spoke of his going as a "little while." He also promised to "come back" to his disciples (see John 14:19, 28). In his coming back only people of faith could "see" him; it was to them that he would give his Spirit. Baptism has gifted us with the Spirit so that with open eyes and open hearts we can see Jesus more clearly in our lives. Growth in Christian faith is a constant deepening of this vision. The Spirit who is a gift and the source of our life is also the one who continually sharpens the focus of our faith. The Spirit is the Spirit of truth whom the world cannot accept, since it neither sees him nor recognizes him. But Jesus says we can recognize him because he remains with us, he is within us (see John 14:17). Jesus spoke of the Spirit-Paraclete at the time of his departure precisely so believers would associate this new presence of God with the life of faith, the "long while" of Christian experience.

The annual celebration of the Easter event is meant to be a deepening and development of our faith in the risen Lord. Throughout the Lenten and Easter seasons the Word of God has focused our attention on the meaning and message of Jesus, on the unique significance of his life, death, and resurrection. Now it is time to refocus on those mysteries in the light of the gift of the Spirit that keeps his message and its meaning alive in our hearts.

During this Easter season, our Gospel is that of John. From the very outset of this witness to the meaning and message of Jesus, we are told that Jesus was marked with the Holy Spirit. It was the Baptist who testified that Jesus is not only filled with the Spirit, "it is he who is to baptize with the Holy Spirit" (John 1:33). The Baptist asserts, "I have seen for myself and have testified, 'This is God's chosen one' " (John 1:34). The same Jesus who rose from the waters of the Jordan alive in the Spirit has risen from the fathomless ocean of death to enliven in the Spirit all who accept him as the chosen one of God. This has been so from the beginning days of the earliest Christian communities. It is the reason for our perennial celebration. "We ourselves announce to you the good news that what God promised our fathers he has fulfilled for us, their children, in raising up Jesus, according to what is written in the second psalm, 'You are my son; this day I have begotten you' " (Acts 13:32-33).

As disciples of the risen Lord, we too have eyes to see and ears to hear; our hearts are filled with faith in God's chosen one. From our experience of Jesus' signs, we now see them in the light of his resurrection. From our hearing of his words, we now interpret them through the power of his Holy Spirit. We are an Easter people. We believe that the risen Lord has breathed his life-giving Spirit on us so that the meaning of his message will remain alive in our hearts. "The Paraclete, the Holy Spirit whom the Father will send in my name, will instruct you in everything, and remind you of all that I told you" (John 14:26). During the Easter season the Church offers us a yearly opportunity to reflect on the source of this living memory. Our Easter Gospel provides us with the annual announcement of the promise and gift of the Spirit-Paraclete.

"Another Paraclete"

At this point a reading of a few sayings about the Spirit-Paraclete will be helpful (John 14:15-17, 25-26; 15:26-27; 16:12-15).

The Paraclete is the term used for the Spirit in the farewell discourse of John's Gospel. Paraclete is the figure of an earthly counselor, companion, or protector. The term itself is borrowed from legal imagery and describes someone who stands by to defend and justify. The Paraclete is more than an advocate. The Paraclete, for Jesus, is the continuation of the complete role he has played on behalf of his disciples. "I will ask the Father and he will give you another Paraclete—to be with you always" (John 14:16). What Jesus has been to the disciples, the Paraclete will continue to be for them. The Paraclete will make permanent what has been temporary in the disciples' relationship with Jesus. The Spirit may be heavenly and of the Father, but like Jesus the mission is of and in the world. The Spirit-Paraclete will have an intimate union with the disciples, a union described by Jesus as being "with" and "in" the disciples (see John 14:17). Like Jesus the Paraclete is a sent gift. Just as Jesus was "God with us," the Spirit will be "Jesus with us."

The Spirit of Truth

The Paraclete is "the Spirit of truth" (John 14:17). Like Jesus the Spirit will lead believers into the way of truth. That is what Jesus meant when he said that the Holy Spirit will "instruct" and "remind" disciples of all that he told them (see John 14:26). The functions of the Spirit are similar to those of the mission of Jesus. Like Jesus the Spirit is sent by the Father.[6] Like Jesus the Spirit teaches and reveals all things.[7] As the Spirit of truth, the Paraclete will continually bring into sharper focus the truth of Jesus, who he is and what he has done. The Spirit is the spirit of the Gospel, a living witness to the Word and deed of Jesus. The Gospel is not a mere recalling; as a work of the Spirit, it is a "living memory." As a work of human hands, it is a faith-filled reflection on the Word and deed of Jesus seen in the light and life of the first communities' post-Easter perspective of the risen Lord.

A New Covenant

The Spirit is the spirit of the covenant, a bond of intimate union between God and his people. Jesus linked the coming of the Spirit with the condition of keeping his commandment and living in union with him (see John 14:15). With this language so reminiscent of the first covenant, Jesus declared the Spirit would be the bonding of a new covenant between God and his people. In the first covenant God said, "If you hearken to my voice and keep my covenant, you shall be my special possession, dearer to me than all other people" (Exod 19:5). Jesus, the Chosen One of God, says, "If you love me and obey the commands I give you, I will ask the Father and he will give you another Paraclete—to be with you always" (John 14:15-16). The Spirit is the fulfillment of the promise spoken by Jeremiah the prophet: "The days are coming, says the Lord, when I will make a new covenant with the house of Israel and the house of Judah" (Jer 31:31), and "I will place my law within them, and write it upon their hearts; I will be their God and they shall be my people" (Jer 31:33). The Spirit is the love bond between God and his people. The Spirit is the constant reminder that in Jesus Christ God has reached out to, taken hold of, and returned with the human embodiment of a people he has chosen to be his own. The Spirit-Paraclete is the permanent spiritual incarnation of the bond that Jesus established with us in the flesh. In us as in Jesus, God and humankind are one. In us as in Jesus, the bonding of that union is the same, the God sent gift of the Holy Spirit.

"Shalom-Peace"

The Spirit is the covenant greeting, the "Shalom of God." That is why the risen Lord anticipated the giving of the Spirit with his greeting of shalom, "Peace be with you" (John 20:19). Jesus' farewell to his disciples is now his greeting and his gift. " 'Peace' is my farewell to you, my peace is my gift to you" (John 14:27). "Peace be with you," Jesus said, "Receive the Holy Spirit" (John 20:21, 22). Jesus' greeting of "Peace" is his conferral of the expected "eternal gift" God promised to his people. It is the love bond that only the Spirit could produce. "I will make with them a covenant of peace; it shall be an everlasting covenant . . . My dwelling shall be with them; I will be their God, and they shall be my people" (Ezek 37:26, 27). What God has promised in his Spirit, he has fulfilled in the flesh of Jesus. What Jesus has promised in the flesh, he has fulfilled in his Spirit. The greeting that the risen Lord received from his Father is the gift he has given to us his disciples. "Shalom-Peace" is not a final farewell signalling a long absence in heaven; it is an eternal gift signifying a permanent presence on earth. "Shalom-Peace," the Spirit-Paraclete, is the eternal love bond between God and his people.

The Witness of Faith

The Spirit initiates believers into the great mysteries of faith, the "indwelling" presence of God, Father, Son, and Holy Spirit within our lives. But initiation is not just indwelling or covenant union. It is a share in divine life, but it is also a share in the mission of Jesus. "As the Father has sent me, so I send you" (John 20:21). "When the Paraclete comes . . . he will bear witness on my behalf. You must bear witness as well" (John 15:26, 27). As disciples we are sent to witness to the truth of Jesus, his meaning and his message, his passion, death, and resurrection. It was Jesus' witness to the truth that led to his rejection and death. It may well be the same for us. The assassinations of Archbishop Romero and the American women in El Salvador and the killing of Father Popieluszko in Poland are all living reminders of this. But Jesus has both forewarned and fortified his disciples. "I have told you all this to keep your faith from being shaken" (John 16:1).

Most of us will never face physical martyrdom because of our faith, but each day of our life in Christ is a challenge to live out the truth of our mission in him. He clearly taught about trial and persecution. Jesus said, "Not only will they expel you from synagogues; a time will come when anyone who puts you to death will claim to be serving God!" (John

16:2). By the time John's Gospel was written, this word about persecution was already being fulfilled. This is reflected in the story of the man born blind. His parents refused to testify on his behalf for fear of being thrown out of the synagogue. At that time it was already agreed "that anyone who acknowledged Jesus as the Messiah would be put out" (John 9:22). When the man who was washed clean of his blindness testified, "If this man were not from God, he could never have done such a thing . . . they threw him out bodily" (John 9:33-34). With new vision the man proclaimed his newfound faith. "I do believe," he said, and he bowed down before the Lord "to worship him" (John 9:38).

The Spirit not only sharpens the focus of our faith in Jesus, but leads us to a life in which we become a witness to him and to his truth. "You must bear witness as well, for you have been with me from the beginning" (John 15:27). The beginnings of our faith brought us to baptism. Baptism was our initiation into a life of union with Jesus and a share in his mission. It unfolds as a never ending journey of witness and worship. It is a life of faith and fidelity, bound up with the presence of the same Spirit that guided the life and mission of Jesus himself. As we reflect upon the challenge of our faith and the gift of the Spirit, we can take comfort from the farewell discourse of Jesus. "Do not be distressed or fearful. You have heard me say, 'I go away for a while, and I come back to you' . . . I tell you this now, before it takes place, so that when it takes place you may believe" (John 14:27, 28, 29).

Texts for Reading

John 14:15-31	The promise of the Spirit-Paraclete
John 16:1-16	The Spirit-Paraclete recalls the meaning and message of Jesus

Suggestions for reflection and/or discussion:

Jesus promised and then gave the Spirit through his passing to the Father. He claimed that by his going away, he would be more present to us than ever before.

1. How does the Spirit keep the meaning and message of Jesus alive for me?
2. What does the term "the witness of faith" mean for me?
3. Does my coming together with other believers for sharing and prayer increase my awareness of the presence of the Spirit? How?

Suggested Prayer Service

Opening Song:	Come Holy Ghost[8]
	O Holy Spirit, by Whose Breath[9]
	Lord, Send Out Your Spirit[10]

Psalm 47 or 111

Reading: Matthew 13:1-23 or Luke 10:21-37

Pause for reflection

Prayer:

Lord Jesus Christ, you have opened the eyes of the blind and the ears of the deaf. Touch our lives with the power of your Spirit that we may see your face and clearly hear your Word. Unite us in your love and send us in your name to bring forth a harvest of good works. We ask this through Christ our Lord. Amen.

Blessing of the Eyes and Ears:

> Following this prayer, the leader, cleric, or catechist invites the people to come up for a

blessing of their eyes and ears.

Touching the eyes and then the ears, the leader prays: "Be open to the Holy Spirit, a spirit of goodness and truth."[11]

Appropriate background music may accompany this action.

When this action is finished all join hands and recite The Lord's Prayer.

Blessing (said by leader):

May the Lord bless us and keep us.
May the Lord make his face shine upon us,
and give us his peace.
May the Lord bless us, Father, Son,
and Holy Spirit.
(All make the Sign of the Cross.)[12]

Exchange a greeting of peace.

Notes

1. Gospel for Tuesday of the first week of Easter.

2. Gospel for the second Sunday of Easter.

3. Preface of the Ascension II.

4. Preface of Pentecost.

5. Preface of the Holy Spirit I.

6. Compare the role of the Spirit in John 14:16, 26 with the mission of Jesus in John 3:16.

7. Compare the teaching role of the Spirit in John 14:26; 16:13 with that of Jesus in John 4:25; 7:14.

8. *People's Mass Book* (New Edition) #84.

9. *Ibid.* #92.

10. *Glory and Praise,* Vol. 3, 88.

11. This is a modification of the RCIA #200-02.

12. There are many blessings that could be used. There are some in the Sacramentary under the heading Solemn Blessings #6-14. The blessings of the catechumens RCIA #121-24 and #374 could also be used as a model for the writing of new blessings for the faithful during the Easter season.

Chapter 7

The Prayer of Jesus
The Seventh Week of Easter

This is the prayer of Jesus: that his disciples may become one as he is one with the Father, Alleluia!
Antiphon for the Communion Rite
Seventh Sunday of Easter

For our final reflection the Easter Gospel draws our attention to the image of Jesus at prayer. The focus of the last week of the Easter season is on the prayer of Jesus from chapter seventeen of John's Gospel. All of the evangelists have scenes of Jesus at prayer. He took part in the formal prayers of his people, both in the synagogue and the temple. He spent long nights in private prayer with the God he called his Father. He taught his disciples how to pray. For Jesus prayer was an expression not only of faith but also of feelings. The Gospels show us a Jesus who knows and expresses himself in both the prayer of agony and defeat as well as at the prayer of praise and thanksgiving.[1] The Gospel of John provides moments and prayers of Jesus not found in the other evangelists: the prayer of Jesus at the tomb of Lazarus, his prayer to the Father for glory, and the long prayer following the farewell discourse.[2] All of these prayers have the solemn address to God as Father and in some way they all reflect the coming of the hour of glory.

At Lazarus' tomb Jesus prayed, "Father, I thank you for having heard me. I know that you always hear me, but I have said this for the sake of the crowd, that they may believe that you sent me" (John 11:41-42). The last sign of the earthly Jesus was the raising of Lazarus. It was, as Jesus said, for the glory of God. Through Lazarus' sickness and death the Son of God revealed himself as the source of resurrection and life (see John 11:4, 25). At the time of his final Passover, Jesus reflected the sentiments of his heart in prayer, "My soul is troubled now, yet what should I say—Father, save me from this hour? But it was for this that I came to this hour. Father, glorify your name!" (John 12:27-28). This is the closest John comes to the sentiments of Jesus in the garden. Yet, despite the note of "trouble" of soul, Jesus prays for his glorification at the time of his hour. It is this prayer that consumes his heart while he is seated at the table of his final meal and farewell discourse. Through his own example of service and self-sacrifice Jesus revealed himself at the table as the source of truth and life. Jesus is our "Teacher" and "Lord." He is the Son of Man in whom God is glorified (see John 13:13, 31).

"The hour has come"

The meal, the discourse, and the final prayer all usher in Jesus' hour of glory. The death of Jesus is his passover to the Father whom he has revealed as light, life, and love. The one great sign of all this is the risen Lord himself whose appearances and presence in our midst confirm and celebrate the truth of his Word and deed. Thus it is the risen Lord, the glorified Son of Man, who leads us in prayer to the Father in heaven. No wonder our Easter celebration and reflections began with his appearances to the first disciples. As present-day disciples, all that we celebrate and all we reflect on is seen in the light of his resurrection and his presence in our midst. It is with this focus of faith that we experience the Easter Gospel. Even when we look back, we see and hear the image and voice of the risen Lord who said, "Blest are they who have not seen and have believed" (John 20:29). It is with our Christian faith, an Easter faith, that we see and hear the Word and deed of Jesus during this season of renewal. What we have seen and heard is the "sign" of the glorified Son of Man, the risen Lord, present in Word, sacrament, and our fellow believers. Through this seeing and hearing, we have come to renewed faith and renewed life in his name. The hour has come; Jesus has revealed the Father's name. He has revealed it and will continue to reveal it, so that God's love for Jesus may live on in us (see John 17:1, 26).

"Give glory to your Son" (John 17:1-8)

The prayer of Jesus at the end of the farewell discourse does many things. It sums up many of his key thoughts and ideas. It reveals the deep desires he had in his heart as he confronted his death. It proclaims his glory as a sharing of life and love with his disciples. And it spans the time zones of his earthly and glorified presence with his disciples. While written in the form of a departing leader's prayer for his followers, it is proclaimed by the risen Lord in the midst of his believing disciples.[3]

During the Book of Signs, Jesus spoke openly to all. The Book of Glory opened with the scene of the supper and the final discourse. There Jesus spoke the intimate thoughts of his heart to his disciples alone. Now, on the threshold of his hour of glory, Jesus speaks not in discourse but in prayer and only to his Father in heaven. This prayer is spoken in the presence of the disciples and so once again they "see" and "hear" Jesus' love for them.

In the first part of his prayer, Jesus reflects upon his mission from the Father and his mission to the disciples. He has glorified the Father by completing the work he was sent to do. Jesus has revealed the name of God; his words and deeds have given a face and a form to God. Jesus' mission was not only to show his disciples what God is like but to share with his followers God's very life. Jesus has revealed our God as a loving shepherd, and as the source of life. He has taught us the closeness of God's relationship with us in revealing God's name. God is Father and source of life. God is "mother" and source of comfort and care. Jesus never used the word "mother" for God. However, the images he employed to describe his relationship to the God he revealed balance a strong, creative, life-giving side with one that is gentle, caring, and nurturing. This is the God Jesus said is the eternal I AM. Jesus said that by knowing him, his followers would share God's eternal life. "Eternal life is this: to know you, the only true God, and him whom you have sent" (John 17:3). We know Jesus in the images he gave us to put a face and form on our God. By our share in these images, we share God's light, life, and love. We know and share with Jesus himself the eternal life of God. This is what the Gospel means by glory. Jesus and the Father are glorified when their life is known and shared. This is the end result of becoming "new creations" in Christ and "abiding" in him. This is the destiny of those who "hear" his voice and who "follow" his way. This is the fruition of those who enjoy a unity of life and love by sharing in the oneness of the vine and the Spirit. This is the message entrusted to and received by believing hearts. "They have known that in truth I came from you," Jesus tells the Father, and of his disciples, he declares, "they have believed it was you who sent me" (John 17:8). This is God's glory. Because of Jesus it is our glory too. It is eternal life!

Jesus has finished the work God gave him to do. His passing to the Father was the "lifting up" that Jesus said would draw all people to himself (see John 12:32). His hour of glory was his going to the Father. His coming back again was his sending of the Spirit into our hearts to continue his mission (see John 20:21-22). The unity of this mystery is described by John in the image of Jesus dying on the cross. "Now it is finished," Jesus said. "Then he bowed his head, and delivered over his spirit" (John 19:30). The same Spirit that was the bond between Jesus and the Father now binds us together in the sharing of one eternal life. No wonder we lift up our hearts with Jesus in prayer and cry out, "Our Father."

"For these I pray" (John 17:9-19)

Jesus described the reason for his prayer and his passage to the Father as the fulfillment of the work God gave him to do. This work was to consecrate his disciples in truth and to share his joy with them. The disciples only gradually understood this as they began to live out the meaning of what Jesus prayed for them on the night before he died. "As you have sent me into the world, so I have sent them into the world" (John 17:18). Through the gift of the Spirit, Jesus sealed the bond that makes his followers a sign of his presence in the world. "It is in them that I have been glorified," Jesus said (John 17:10). Jesus has given us his word, his Spirit and his joy. This is the meaning of his resurrection greeting, "Peace, be with you" (see John 20:19-22). Jesus has prayed for us to the Father. He has prayed that we be kept safe, cared for, nourished, and guarded from the evil one. He has prayed that we will remain faithful in moments of darkness, even in death itself.

In the Gospels there are two traditions surrounding Jesus' prayer after the Last Supper. The Gospels other than John picture Jesus in the garden seeking support from his disciples as he prostrates on the ground to pray. There Jesus' prayer is one of agony and supplication, a prayer to the Father that his will be done.[3] John pictures Jesus praying with head raised to heaven seated at table with those for whom he prays—a very different image. We know there was an agony in the garden and a death on the cross. But we also know that because of this, God's will has been done and Jesus' prayer has been answered. As risen Lord, Jesus supports us in our gardens and on our crosses. He does not ask that we be taken out of the world, only that we be guarded from the evil one. He sends us, as he has been sent, to continue his presence and his prayer—"Thy kingdom come, thy will be done."

"Through their word" (John 17:20-26)

Jesus' prayer as his hour of glory began was for those at table who had heard his word. It was also a prayer for disciples of all ages, those who have heard the first disciples' word and witness to Jesus and passed it on. Jesus has prayed and continues to pray for us, his present-day disciples. His prayer is for our growth in unity and faith.

As he drew his life and his prayer to conclusion, Jesus revealed the depth of his love for all who come to faith in him. He prayed that our life and union in him will become the very union and life he shares with his Father, "I pray that they may be [one] in us . . . I living in them, you living in me" (John 17:21, 23). Like the union of the image of the vine and the branches, Jesus prays that we will share one life, one love in the unity that exists in God, a communion and community of Father, Son, and Holy Spirit. There is no greater love, no greater life than this. As disciples, believers in Christ, and baptized members of his glorified body, we are not only drawn into a communion with God through Jesus, we are drawn and integrated into the very unity of life and love which is God. This is the meaning and the depth of Jesus' constant prayer, "Father, all those you gave me I would have in my company where I am, to see this glory of mine . . . Just Father, . . . to them I have revealed your name, and I will continue to reveal it so that your love for me may live in them, and I may live in them" (John 17:24, 25, 26).

Living the Mystery

As we draw our reflections and the Easter season to a close, we find ourselves in mystery. It is, however, a mystery that is not absent or remote. It is as present as the image of God found in his Word and in the face of the risen Christ. It is as close as the baptized Christian next to us. It is the mystery we live and experience as the "new creations" we are becoming through baptism. It is the mystery we live and express each time we celebrate the table prayer to our Father that Jesus has given us. We live out our baptism by our lives of union with God and with one another. The meaning of that "new creation" increases and multiplies each time we celebrate and commune in the presence of the risen Christ at the Eucharist. Baptism is unrepeatable, but initiation into Christ continues to unfold with each breath, each prayer, each good deed, each Eucharist. The Eucharist is the table prayer where the word and deed of Jesus are ever present to "see" and "hear" once again. The Eucharist is the "abiding in" that Jesus promised when he spoke of his life and his love as a vine united to its branches. The Eucharist is the sending of the Spirit to bind us together in one communion of life. The Eucharist is both the table prayer and the daily bread Jesus gave us on the night before he entered his glory. This is the mystery we celebrate in the Church's prayer of praise:

> Father, all-powerful and ever-living God, we do well always and everywhere to give you thanks through Jesus Christ our Lord.

> At the last supper, as he sat at table with his apostles, he offered himself to you as the spotless lamb, the acceptable gift that gives you perfect praise. Christ has given us this memorial of his passion to bring us its saving power until the end of time.

> In this great sacrament you feed your people and strengthen them in holiness, so that the family of mankind may come to walk in the light of one faith, in one communion of love.

> We come then to this wonderful sacrament to be fed at your table and grow into the likeness of the risen Christ.[4]

As we live the mystery of our baptism, the union of our lives in God through Christ's Spirit, and live the mystery of the Eucharist, the sharing of with others through Christ's Spirit, we continue to pray as Jesus has taught us, "Our Father . . . ," always believing that our prayer and our lives are becoming an eternal "Amen."

Texts for Reading

John 17:1-26   Prayer for faith and unity

Suggestions for reflection and/or discussion:

Jesus is risen and present to the Father. He continues to make intercession for us. Through the Easter gift of the Spirit he joins us to the Father and calls us to join him in prayer.

1. Does my prayer reflect my union with the Father?
2. Does my prayer express a relationship to God as gentle and compassionate, the motherly side of God?
3. Do I use the Lord's Prayer as a guide to personal prayer?
4. How is my life a living "amen" to the Eucharistic Prayer:
   Through him,
   with him,
   in him,
   in the unity of the Holy Spirit, all glory and honor is yours, almighty Father,
   forever and ever_____?

Suggested Prayer Service

Opening Song: Father, We Thank Thee[5]

We Thank You, Father[6]

The Lord's Prayer is our common family prayer to our Father in heaven, the Father of our Lord, Jesus Christ. The Lord's Prayer is also a lesson on how to pray. As we listen to the words of Jesus offering us this prayer once again, let us hear it as it was heard the first time, a response to the request "Lord, teach us to pray."

Readings: Matthew 6:5-15 or Luke 11:1-13

Pause for reflection

Now recite the Lord's Prayer line by line, pausing to let people express briefly what each phrase means to them:

Our Father,
who art in heaven,
hallowed be thy name;
Thy Kingdom come;
Thy will be done on earth as it is in heaven.
Give us this day our daily bread;
and forgive us our trespasses
as we forgive those who trespass against us;
and lead us not into temptation,
but deliver us from evil.
For the kingdom, the power, and the glory are yours,
now and forever.
Amen.

Final Prayer:

Father, as we draw to a close this Easter season of new life in Christ, help us to share what we have received. Renew us in your Spirit and continue to form us in the image of your risen Son who is forever the light of the world. We ask this through Christ our Lord. Amen.

Exchange a greeting of Peace.

Notes

1. For a selection of texts that show the many moods of Jesus' prayer, see Matt 6:5-13; 26:36-46; Mark 1:35; 15:34; Luke 2:41-52; 10:21-22; 22:14-20.

2. For these prayers of Jesus, see John 11:41-42; 12:27-28; 17:1-26.

3. For other prayers of departing leaders, see those of Moses in Deut 32, 33; Samuel in 1 Sam 12; and Paul in Acts 20:17-38.

4. This prayer of Jesus is found in the other three Gospels. See Mark 14:32-42; Matt 26:36-46; Luke 22:39-46.

5. Preface of the Holy Eucharist, II.

6. *People's Mass Book* (New Edition) #121.

7. *Glory and Praise,* Vol. 3 #272.

Conclusion

Pentecost and Beyond

On the final day of the great Easter feast, the Church prayerfully reminds us that it has taken fifty days to celebrate the fullness of the mystery of God's love revealed in Jesus. We pray in thanksgiving for the gift of new life we have received in baptism, and we ask that God will continue to strengthen us with his light and the gift of the Holy Spirit. We also pray that the events of Easter and Pentecost will be not just memories but a living experience in our minds and hearts. The resurrection of Jesus and his sending of the Spirit are what Christianity are all about. Easter and Pentecost are not just a yearly season; they are meant to be a way of life.

In calling the Second Vatican Council Pope John XXIII prayed for the renewal of Christian life. The image he gave us for that renewal was "a new Pentecost." Today we are still trying to live out the challenge of that image and prayer. Pentecost is that challenge. Pentecost means to receive the gift of Christ's life and Spirit and to share it with others. Pentecost is the constant unfolding of the Church's Easter prayer: arise and renew!

One contemporary response to the challenge of renewal is the Church's process for incorporating new adult members, the Rite of Christian Initiation of Adults (RCIA). Through this process of experience and instruction, those who seek new life and faith remind all who are baptized in Christ that Christian life is a continual call to conversion of heart and increase of faith. As candidates for baptism, catechumens remind us of the need for renewal of life. As newborn Christians they are a sign of our own risen life in Christ. The Adult Rite of Initiation is giving a renewed prominence to the Easter season. It is a time when all Christians, new and veteran believers alike, are called to celebrate and reawaken to the mystery of their lives in Christ. This Period of Mystagogy, as it is called, is a time to reflect on and experience once again the person and the power of the risen Lord. He is the Easter Gospel. Its meaning and message will only be realized if we live out the heart of the Christian experience by knowing Christ and sharing the power that flows from his resurrection (see Phil 3:10).

The images found in the Easter Gospel have provided us with seven weeks of prayerful reflection on the risen Christ and how he shares his light and life with us. As living water and bread from heaven, Jesus refreshes and nourishes his flock. As Good Shepherd Jesus shows us the way to eternal truth and life. As the vine that gives life and bears abundant fruit, Jesus has entwined his call and his challenge in one living union called discipleship. Through the gift of his Spirit, Jesus has empowered us to answer that call and to meet the challenge by sharing his life and love with others. It is only through the gift of the Spirit that we can ever keep Jesus' commandment, "love one another as I have loved you" (John 15:12). It is only through the presence of the Paraclete that we can live the mission Christ has given us, "As the Father has sent me, so I send you" (John 20:21). The Easter Gospel, like all the good news, is a call and a commission. It is a way of life that can only be lived and sustained through reflection and prayer. Only these provide the inspiration and strength that is needed to make us loving witnesses and willing servants of the risen Lord.

This book has been a series of reflections on the Easter Gospel found in the Church's Lectionary for the Easter season. These reflections have put us in contact with the event of Easter and the experience of Pentecost. The event of Pentecost, which is recorded in the Acts of the Apostles, evokes another set of images and reflections. The Gospel centers on Christ. The Acts center on the followers of Christ, the Church. Both show the meaning of sharing God's light and life with others. Like Christ the followers of Christ, who make up his body, the Church, are meant to be "a light to the nations." This is the opening thought and the guiding vision of the Second Vatican Council's teaching in its Constitution on the Church, "Lumen Gentium."

The Church is a body of believers rising to new life in the Spirit of Christ. Just as Easter announces the resurrection, pushing Christ out from the tomb and into the world of human events in a new and dynamic way, Pentecost proclaims the renewal of the Christian people, nudging us beyond our present stage of growth out into an increasingly complex world that craves the witness and the service that only a believer in Jesus can give. Yes, Christ is risen, and the proof of it is the life-giving and faith-filled service of his followers. Through us Pentecost lives on!

Like Nicodemus who came forth from darkness into the light as a minister to the body of Christ, believer-disciples are meant to come forth from the Easter experience to share Christ's light and life in a ministry of service to the Church. At the conclusion of the Easter season in the final Eucharist of Pentecost, the Easter Candle is once again carried in procession through the Church. This symbol of Christ, "the Light of the World," is placed in the baptistry near the font where Church is born and annually renewed. There it stands, a shining beacon of light and hope. Like Christ risen from the tomb, Christian believers are empowered through the Easter mysteries to let their light shine. Christian life is not only a call to hear and reflect the message of the Easter Gospel; it is a commission in the Spirit to be a living image of the risen Lord himself.

Fr. Malcolm Cornwell, a member of the Passionist Congregation, was ordained in 1969 and did graduate studies at St. John's University, Collegeville, Minnesota, in liturgy and spirituality. His pastoral experience includes the preaching of parish renewal weeks and retreats to laity, religious, and priests. He is a team member of the Emmaus Spirituality Program for priestly renewal, an associate member of the North American Academy of Liturgy, and a member of the North American Forum on the Catechumenate. A contributor to pastoral journals, he is the author of the book *Formed by His Word.* Father Cornwell resides at the Calvary Retreat Center, Shrewsbury, Massachusetts. He is a member of the liturgical commissions for the diocese of Worcester and for the eastern province of the Passionist Congregation.